Jeff Sutherland
Rini van Solingen
Eelco Rustenburg

THE POWER *of* SCRUM

ISBN: 1463578067
ISBN-13: 9781463578060
Library of Congress Control Number: 2011909743

CreateSpace, North Charleston, SC

Foreword to The Power of Scrum

...

If there was a Nobel Prize for management, and if there was any justice in the world, I believe that the prize would be awarded, among others, to Jeff Sutherland, Ken Schwaber, and Mike Cohn for their contributions to the invention of Scrum.

Over more than a decade, software development teams using Scrum have been extraordinarily productive. The best teams routinely obtain productivity increases of 200 to 400 percent, changes that are industry-disruptive in scale. When firms like Salesforce.com have implemented Scrum boldly, the financial results have been remarkable, i.e. with more than 40% annual growth for the whole firm.

But what is Scrum? In one sense, Scrum is the simplest idea under the sun: find out what the clients really want and continuously deliver that to them sooner. The problem is that implementing this simple idea means unlearning most of what today's managers know for certain, things that are taught in every business school and assumed as fundamental truths in most management textbooks.

Scrum is not just a set of tools, or a new business process, or an engineering framework for software development. It involves a fundamental transformation of the way work is managed. It involves a new way of thinking, speaking, and acting in the workplace for both managers and those doing the work.

How do you communicate a fundamentally new way of thinking, speaking, and acting, while simultaneously getting people to shed a large part of what they are sure they already know?

Attempting to accomplish this by offering reasons and arguments typically leads to counter-reasons and more arguments.

By contrast, telling a story can spark the imagination and generate creativity, interaction, and transformation. Readers can begin to imagine what implementing Scrum would be like for them.

The Power of Scrum is such a story. It translates dry and abstract reasons and numbers into a compelling living picture of what Scrum involves.

It tells a tale of how Scrum came to be successfully introduced in a software development company. The tale rings true: it feels authentic because, unlike what you read in most management textbooks, the people in this book are the mixed bag that you find in any real-life workplace: educated, intelligent, and at times collaborative but also opinionated, egotistical, jealous, and proud. Trust is at a premium. Snake-oil and management fads are rampant. Employees have lives outside the workplace with spouses who have different agendas. This is the kind of a world where a manager might throw a laptop into the drywall to make a point he felt strongly about.

In this refreshing, energizing, and persuasive tale, you will live through the introduction of Scrum in a software development firm. You will experience that world through the eyes of Mark, the Chief Technology Officer, and get a holistic account of the change process.

The story is entertaining and moving, memorable and authentic. Through it, you will see the meaning of Scrum. You will get both the feel of it and the why of it. In the process, you will learn how you too can radically transform the way work in your firm is managed and so get the extraordinary benefits that flow from continuous innovation, deep job satisfaction and client delight.

Stephen Denning
Author of *The Leader's Guide to Radical Management* (Jossey-Bass, 2010) and The Leader's Guide to Storytelling (Jossey-Bass, 2nd ed, 2011)

Foreword by the Authors

...

Since the initial publishing of the Scrum framework in 1995 by Jeff Sutherland and Ken Schwaber, Scrum has been used all over the world as the Agile method of choice for thousands of companies. Scrum has evolved to be the de-facto standard for Agile processes. Scrum is now spreading beyond IT product development, into non-IT areas, such as sales and marketing, where teamwork can get more work done faster with higher quality.

The initial idea behind Scrum was to unleash the potential of software professionals. The challenge was to have teams collaborating to empower themselves to bootstrap into a high performing state. The goal was to simultaneously inspire high productivity, continuous innovation, deep job satisfaction and client delight. Most organizations have learned by experience, during the last decades, that software projects cannot be completely planned in advance. Changing requirements and progressive insights largely impact project plans and cause them to fail completely or to cause major delays and budget overruns. Scrum gives control of the value stream back to the business. It supports business in rapid, short-cyclic value creation and supports people in using their talents to the utmost.

We, the authors, are asked frequently to explain how Scrum works and why it works. Explaining that is fun, but also indicates that 'what', 'how', and, 'why' are not clear by themselves. We felt we had to come up with another way. So we decided to write a business fable about Scrum following the footsteps of authors such as Goldratt, Lencioni, Denning, and Chowdhury.

In this book, we provide an easy to read story that explains **what** Scrum is, **how** it works, and **why** it works. The book can be read completely in less than 3 hours. The story is told from the point of view of Mark Resting, CTO at Logistrux, a software product company. With the support of a Scrum coach, he successfully changes the way in which his organization works, at the same time using his experience with Scrum to address a private dilemma. The personal dynamics and the flow of the change towards Scrum give a good idea of the ups and downs of introducing Scrum and what it can come to mean for an organization. The story, although fictional, is credible and provides an entertaining way to get to know and understand Scrum.

With this story, we hope to contribute to the successful deployment of Scrum in practice. We hope that readers gain an understanding and appreciation of Scrum, and that the book helps their first encounters with Scrum be more successful. We know it will work in the IT industry. We are confident it will work outside IT too.

Jeff Sutherland, Rini van Solingen and Eelco Rustenburg
The Netherlands, September 17, 2011

Table of Contents

...

Chapter 1:
London

...

Man, what a day. Not the worst day of my life, but up there. Top five.

The rain was falling in sheets as I dashed from the doors to the taxi—only a few feet, but enough time for me to get completely soaked. This day was only getting better.

The door handle was slick with rain and I struggled with it, my hand slipping clumsily as I attempted to wrench open the door. Feeling the water slide deeper down my neck, I braced myself—and put my foot right into a puddle, the water seeped into my socks and around my toes. I imagined the long flight back to DC in a soggy suit and wet shoes. Wonderful.

My headache reminded me of its presence as we pulled away from Logistrux headquarters. "Heathrow," I said. "American Airlines."

My body still wasn't sure what time it was. My stomach was tight. My back was aching in new and interesting places. My mind was reeling. We were in trouble. Big trouble.

It had been one of those friendly, but not so friendly invitations the English are so damned good at. "Would you be so kind as to attend a meeting tomorrow from 1 to 5 in the afternoon here in London?" the president's private secretary had asked me in one of those so clipped and polite accents.

I'd looked at the clock, thanked God for time differences, and managed as enthusiastically as I could muster, "I'd be happy to." Just enough time to go home, grab my passport and some clothes, and explain to Anne that I'd be out of the country for a day. This wasn't the first time she'd heard last-minute travel plans; life as a CTO seems to require them. I didn't wait for her complaints to reach me. Before she could start a fight, I was already out the door.

I'd never been to Logistrux HQ before. I hadn't really seen the need. Well, I'd met them at last. I suppose when you have to postpone a product release by three months for the *second* time, people start to sit up and take notice.

I'd dreaded the meeting the whole flight over, barely getting any sleep. I had known it would be tough. I had known they wouldn't be happy. I'd had no idea *how* unhappy they were. It hadn't been a fun afternoon.

I flipped through my notes as the suburbs of London blurred by through the rain. No need really; I already knew what I'd promised. Three months. A last chance. I don't think they'd have even given me that if they hadn't sunk so much money and time into this project already. The software had to be delivered in three months. No more wiggle room, no last-minute delays, no 'few more days.' Three months.

I looked at my watch. It was September 18th. We had until a week before Christmas. There went any thought of Thanksgiving with Anne's family. We'd have to go on a 'death march.' I decided not to send her a text message with that news, thinking I'd better wait for the right time to tell her cautiously.

Even with that, could we get it done? I had no idea. I dashed off a quick note on my phone to Rick as the cab rounded a corner, roaming charges be damned. "Enjoy your weekend. It'll be your last for a while. Last chance at Logistrux. Delivery on 12/18."

Rick knows the deal. He's been a project manager for years. I trust him. He'd done bigger projects than this. Of course, he was also the guy who had said two months was all we needed when I asked for another three months last time. I had thought I'd given us enough time to be safe. *It'll be fine*, I'd thought.

It hadn't been, not by a long shot. The president of Logistrux made exactly that point to me a few hours ago; he made it painfully clear. There'd been no yelling, but I felt like I'd been very carefully skinned and mounted under glass.

We couldn't afford to fail. Logistrux was our biggest client.

How in the world can I guarantee release in three months? I asked myself. I'd just promised that, but for the life of me I couldn't figure out how.

I sloshed toward the check-in desk. I had an hour. That should've been enough time, right? The American Airlines agent looked at me with some pity. "Hurry," she motioned toward the gates, "You might make it."

I gazed at the unbroken line of tired business folk tapping on PDAs, families stuffing their precious fluids into plastic bags, the elderly tourists struggling to take off their shoes. At that moment, as I slowly dripped my way to the back of the line, I knew it was hopeless. But I went through the motions anyway, slouching my way through the security theater that is our last line of defense against what exactly, no one has made clear.

I emerged from stage left holding my shoes and belt in one hand and half-open luggage in the other as I did the wettest sprint on record. Sadly, my award-winning time just wasn't good enough; I slid into the gate only to see that the doors were already closed. I surprised the gate agents enough that I actually watched them paint on the plastic smiles that say any argument is futile. They quite pleasantly offered to put me on the next available flight. The next day. At four.

Fortunately, the airport hotel had a clothing store and great water pressure.

The bar was charming, at least. All dark wood and leather. I wondered if they'd built it just so they'd have a filming location for 'lovely English bar,' only using it as one in between shots, to help pay its rent.

I felt somewhat refreshed. The shower had helped, as did the dry clothes. A light meal had worked wonders on the headache. Now I needed a few drinks so I could stop thinking for a little while about any impossible promises some foolish CTO might have made.

I ordered a pint of Courage, thinking maybe I could use some.

"Cheers!" The man at the corner of the bar raised his glass. Big, burly guy. Looked like he used to be a football player, though that would have been pre-ponytail and a few decades ago.

"There are some constants in the universe at least," I grinned back at him. "Any bar in Europe and there's an American drinking beer alone."

"Well, they make it right here. At home it's like making love in a canoe," he chuckled.

"It can be close to water. Mark Resting." I offered my hand.

"Jerry."

"California?"

"How'd you guess?"

I nodded to his shirt. "A shirt that loud would get you arrested back East."

"And the blue shirt and khakis?" He gestured toward my attire.

"In DC they issue them to you at birth."

Jerry, it turned out, had a flight to San Francisco the next day. "What are you doing in London?"

He was cheerful. He was on his way back home after presenting a paper at a conference in the Netherlands—something on the use of "Scrum" in developing video games.

I thought to myself, *I'm the CTO of a software firm, and developers are good sports, but not usually full contact types.*

And that's when I asked the question that, in retrospect, changed my entire life. "What does rugby have to do with developing software?"

"I'll tell you, Mark," Jerry waved his now empty pint glass, "but only if you buy me another beer."

Chapter 2:
Scrum

...

"To use a rough analogy: in the game of rugby the players form into a group called the scrum and try to get control of the ball so that their team can run with it and score. They pass the ball back and forth to each other to gain momentum going down the field. In our version of the game, the ball represents ideas, and the scrum is simply called 'Scrum.'" Jerry looked directly at me. "Our Scrum is a process, a method, a way of thinking about how we do stuff. You're in the software business; you've heard of 'Agile' processes?"

"Sure."

"But you have no idea what that means, do you? It's just a buzzword to you, something people throw about at meetings. You'll show how agile you are by doing something better and faster, right?"

"Well…" I said, remembering a time or two I might have been guilty of throwing lots of words at my clients to make them feel better.

"Just think about the word for a second. Forget what you've heard about it. What does it mean?"

"Quick?"

"It can mean that, but it can also mean flexible or adaptable. And that's the meaning of Scrum. When people talk about Agile, they often think that you'll just work faster. With Scrum you *can* become faster, but that isn't the main purpose. The purpose of Scrum is to increase your *agility*."

"I'm not quite sure I get it," I admitted. That wasn't easy for me; I'm usually convinced I'm one of the smartest guys in the room.

"Okay. In a nutshell, what Scrum forces you to do is to always be open to adapting your priorities. And if your prior-

ities change, your product changes. These priorities are set by new insights and ideas, both from yourself and your client. At the same time, you're working in short, predictable development cycles—say two weeks. And at the end of that time you deliver something to your client: a new working version of your product. Each time, like clockwork. So your client is seeing what you're doing *all the time*, and they can see how your product is improving each and every moment. They're constantly giving you feedback on your product. **It's a true collaboration, which constantly makes your product better. And as the quality of your product improves, so does your credibility with your clients.**"

Jerry paused then for a moment, taking a swig of ale, "And what is credibility based on?"

"Your reputation?"

"And what is your reputation based on? One thing. One thing only. It's simple, but for a lot of companies it's hard. Do you keep your promises? When you say something is going to be done, is it done? Are you a man of your word?"

Looking down, I guiltily thought back to the extensions I'd had to ask Logistrux for. Each time I'd promised them that this time it would be different. Each time I'd failed to live up to my promises. This was my last chance. My credibility was in tatters with them. I looked back up at Jerry. He looked me in the eye and nodded.

"It's important to keep your promises in life, Mark, and in business. You must see this all the time: companies that can't deliver predictably. From the look on your face, I'll guess your company can't do it."

"Not all the time; some of the time. I mean, we try…we're not a bad company."

"Of course not." Jerry smiled. "Of course not. But I bet Scrum can help you. Scrum makes you keep your promises. It brings things under control, makes things transparent both to you and to your customer. It forces you to be honest with yourself, your company, and your client."

Jerry chuckled warmly. "And, Mark, you're going to think I'm crazy. But we can make the world a better place."

"Really?"

"Really. Think about it: If software development becomes effective for the first time, if we consistently deliver only what we need and it's better… Think of the savings—in time, money, the electricity, and heck, even the paper that would have printed up reams of specs that were constantly being revised. Adapting in real time to deliver exactly what is needed allows us to make more for less. Maybe that's a bit too green for you, but it allows us to become more sustainable."

I glanced quickly at his ponytail, but checked myself before teasing him about it. His passion was obvious.

"That sustainability also applies to developers, Mark. Scrum allows us to create a sustainable pace for our work."

I quickly thought about the e-mails I'd already sent warning people of the coming 'death march.' If Scrum could alleviate that even a little, it'd be worth it.

"Furthermore," Jerry continued, "Scrum makes the developers fully responsible. It empowers them. They are in complete control of their own working processes. Their own opinions are more important than 'standard' development procedures. The focus of the team is to deliver a fully working product. That's what it's all about, right? Everything else—documentation, whatever—everything else is secondary to delivering a working product."

"Jerry," I objected, "c'mon. I've had to move mountains to introduce a standard development process at more than one company. Are you trying to convince me that isn't necessary? If developers can just do what *they* think is important, and they don't document anything, it'll turn into chaos, quickly—very 'gile.'"

Jerry straightened up and bounced back. "I just explained. Scrum doesn't mean fast. It means getting more done with less work. If this is how you listen to your customers, I'll tell you how successful your company is!"

He smiled then, showing his teeth. "No. No chaos here, Mark. Scrum really works. It almost seems like magic at times. I'm serious; it works that well. In the past, oh, twenty years or so, we've learned that software requirements are never complete and always changing. That's the nature of reality. We can't change it. Don't fight it; embrace it. Work *with* change. That's what Scrum does. And by responding to change constantly, we can bring business value."

He raised one hand to gesture broadly. "Think about it. In traditional development approaches that idea has never been incorporated. Why, that would upset all the plans, all the budgets. Adjusting scope or modifying requirements? That's a no-go. People think that blocking requirements changes is the only way to control budget, scope, and time."

"And they're wrong, Mark." He placed his hands flat on the bar. "They aren't bad people, just like you're not, not really. But when they try so hard to limit themselves, to stick to the plan, to *not* have changes, they can't keep their promises. Things change whether we like it or not."

He looked at me again. "But what if there was a better way? A way of working that actually encourages changes? Every time there's a new release of software, more ideas become clear, new ways of doing things, or new things you need. So, to be really successful, you have to be willing to improve everything based on those new insights."

"Look at it this way, Mark." He paused, sipped his beer. "In our work we always talk about a *change* in requirements. But really, it's an *improvement*. **If the client, or the user, wants a change, they don't do it to make things worse. They do it to make things better. It's highly desirable, from a business point of view, to take those requests very seriously and give them a central place in your process. Scrum does that; it follows the rhythm of business process improvement at its core.** All software does, after all, is make that business process more effective or more efficient."

I nodded. He had a point. If you knew there were going to be a lot of changes, you really should plan for how you were going to tackle them. When we started the Logistrux project, nobody knew *exactly* what we were going to make. The concept of what they wanted sounded good. We all had faith in it. But we couldn't *precisely* predict how the new features would be used, let alone all the functional details those features would require. There was no other product like it on the market. That meant we had to spend a lot of time defining *exactly* what it would do. We did user interviews, and we learned that different users saw different ways of using the product.

"You know what's funny, Jerry?"

"What?"

"I'm here in London meeting with a client who is not happy."

"I guessed."

"And when we started this project for them, we knew we didn't know precisely what we were going to do."

"Umm-hmm."

"And yet we then went ahead and made a timeline for the entire project. It seems quite strange in retrospect. After all, we *knew* the project would never go according to that plan. They never do. Were we just fooling ourselves?"

"Yep."

"Rick, my project manager, he made the plan. It was a project, after all; that's what project managers *do*. The client wants a plan; how do they know *when* they're getting *what* if they don't have one?"

"Well…"

"No, wait. Let me talk this through for a sec. So, this company we're working for: in the first year *alone* they had three big change requests. One of them was so fundamental we had to basically start over from scratch. We had spent months and lots of meetings getting a good idea of what we needed to do to make what they wanted happen. But we just couldn't cope with that much change. The deadline…the one I had *promised* we would meet…we couldn't."

I took a quick swallow of beer. "But if we did it your way…if we embraced changing everything all the time, we couldn't meet our objective either. If we did what you're saying, we wouldn't know what we'd get in the end, no? It's like I want to go to Rome on vacation, but if I use this Scrum approach there's a chance I could end up in Berlin!"

"Exactly!" Jerry shouted. "Just imagine. You think you want to go to Rome on vacation. See the Coliseum, eat some Italian food, drink some good wine. But what if you tested your wishes regularly? Really thought about what you wanted to do on vacation? And then you end up in Berlin. Well, doesn't that mean you never really wanted to go to Rome after all? It's fine. With your traditional way of planning it all out from the beginning, you'd arrive in Rome, go tour the Vatican, all the time wishing you were drinking from a stein in a beer garden!"

I stopped with my beer halfway to my mouth. He was right, I realized. With my approach I would end up where I'd set out to go, but not where I actually wanted to go. The same was true of Logistrux. Our software is only of value when it does what our clients actually want it to do: add value to their business. What they thought in a meeting room a year before is actually irrelevant.

"But how does it work?" I carefully placed my pint on the bar. "I can't just tell my customers, 'We'll see when it's finished.' They'd laugh in my face. They want to know when they're going to get their product. It's as simple as that."

"And that's why," Jerry said quietly, "you have to give them a new version of your product every month. You don't let them wait for years."

"Every month?" Incredulously I turned toward him. "We're having problems doing a release a year! Once a month? I don't even want to think about the problems we'd have. We wouldn't spend any time developing; we'd just be testing and fixing bugs."

Jerry looked at me intently as he said, "You're wrong, Mark. Every month, more often if possible. They need to get a working version every month. **It may seem difficult at first, but you'll get better at it. How do you get to Carnegie Hall? Practice. Practice. Practice. It's the only way to get good."**

"And companies are actually doing this right now?"

"Many companies using Scrum work with a two-week cycle, some even with a one-week cycle! The key is that when you release all the time, the amount of change from one to the next is never very large. So there's not much that can go wrong. Think about it: how much easier is it to fix a bug that a developer wrote yesterday than one he created ten months ago?"

"A lot. He still has the whole thing in his head. He doesn't have to try and remember what he was thinking when he wrote the code."

"Exactly. I can barely remember what I ate for dinner yesterday. It's a rare developer that can remember what they built and how they built it half a year ago."

"And— " he brought up one finger dramatically. "And, the added value—and Scrum is all about added value—is that you eventually understand how much work you can get done in a given time frame. That makes it easier for you to keep your promises. You become much better at estimating the amount of work you can handle. It's also easier to plan ahead four weeks than it is a year."

He stopped for a moment, looked at me, and smiled sadly. "How often do you break your promises? How often do you have to delay your releases?"

Too often, I thought, as my stomach clenched. I tried the same line on Jerry that I'd used variations of all too many times that day. "Software development is unpredictable. Sometimes it might be a few months late. You always encounter the unexpected."

"Okay," said Jerry. "I'll accept that as a given. But what if, in the event of a setback, you could just fall back to a working product only two weeks old? Sure, some functionality wouldn't be there, but most of it would be! If you have something to postpone, it will be there after the next cycle, only two weeks. Wouldn't that be useful?"

"Yeah, yeah, but…" I drifted off for a second, thinking. This just seemed like chaos. We'd spent months getting all of the Logistrux ideas clear. It was a win-win for us; Logistrux was our biggest client, but not our only one, and what they wanted we could then sell to everyone else. A generic extension paid for by the customer. How perfect was that?

This Scrum thing seemed just too abstract, too academic. That was no way to run a developmental environment; you would waste time making all those releases instead of developing new features.

I looked at Jerry, who was gazing expectantly at me with one eyebrow raised. I hate that trick. I tried for years to master it, but I just can't separate one eyebrow from the other. I held a finger up and thought as I took a sip of beer.

Jerry smiled at me as I shook my head. "I know what you're thinking."

"It just doesn't seem...okay." I paused. "Okay, let me ask you some questions. For example, in the beginning we have to spend a couple months just figuring out what the customer actually wants. We don't have the level of detail to release anything."

Jerry responded immediately. "It's simple, Mark. You only work out the detail of those parts of the system you are certain are necessary and that the client clearly wants. These are the highest priorities with the greatest value for the client. Because they're so important, they'll also be the most clear. It's almost a law that the main purpose of any new system will be the most obvious, so you should work on that first. Here's what you do: at just the right time, you work out the detailed design of one part of the system, whatever the highest priority is. Build it. Test it. And then deliver it. Then you sit down with the client to decide what the next highest priority is. And that will become clearer because they already have your working software to play with."

He leaned forward on his stool; his face became more animated. He moved his hands smoothly, emphasizing his points. "The first part is letting go. Let go of figuring out everything beforehand, because you can't; it's impossible. Anything changes and you're back at square one. Instead, work with your client. Figure out what is most important to him or her that you can build and deliver in, say, a month. Then after that cycle is done, you sit down again and see if it really adds the value your client expected and whether you really understood what they want. In Scrum, we call each of those cycles a Sprint."

"A 'Sprint'?"

"Sure. Here's what you do: For each Sprint choose the most essential thing that, according to your customer, adds the most value. That way, with each and every Sprint you bring the product one step further in the direction that adds the most value. At the end of each Sprint you're getting feedback from the customer. And think about it: if you messed up, you'll know within a month. How long does it usually take you to get feedback from a customer?"

"Well, we deliver a release once, maybe twice a year. That's pretty typical." I said.

"Too long! If you wait that long, the feedback you get will have way too much to deal with at once. You won't be able to process that amount of feedback, or at least, you won't want to. More likely you'll start suggesting 'work-arounds.' That just gets people used to flaws that you've created. Not good. When you deliver only small changes, you get feedback that's small enough to actually deal with and fix the problems. Worst case scenario: you throw away a single Sprint. But come on, two or four weeks? Who cares? A year? Then you care!"

"And," he said before I could comment, "You have a job for your customer. He needs to be deeply involved. Ideally, he should be at the development site to help guide the developers. They're the ones who know what needs to be done, after all. Developers are good at developing software, but not good at understanding the totality of the customer's business needs."

At that point I raised my hand. "Wait just a minute. Are you kidding? My customers have better things to do, and a lot of them live on the other side of the planet. They don't have time to hang around our developers. That's what they pay us for."

"That sounds good," said Jerry, "But think about it, if customers aren't willing to invest time and energy in developing a product that they say they need, well, they should ask themselves if it really matters to them. If it's important, then they'll be willing to invest the time. After all, it will return them more than the investment. If they aren't willing, then you shouldn't be working with them. It's just not that important."

Jerry stopped for a second. He shook his head, moving his grey ponytail back and forth once. "Here's how I explain this to customers. I tell them, 'You have a vision in your head of what you want. Isn't it important for the software developers to understand *exactly* what you want? And to do that they have to understand *why* you want it. If that's not understood, it's highly unlikely they'll actually make what you need. Over and over I hear that software developers don't understand the customer. Okay, let's take that as a given. Doesn't that indicate that *you* as a customer have failed to do your work well? Isn't it *your* responsibility to work closely with the developers so *you* can steer them toward what *you* need? Well, that means frequent and close contact. If you, as a customer, don't think it's worth that level of investment, then the project isn't that valuable to you, is it? Why are you spending your money on it? You shouldn't even start the project in that case.'"

Jerry paused for breath, obviously not quite finished. I quickly interjected before he could go off again, "Hold up. I don't work for one client. I work for dozens. Or for myself really. I'm developing software I can sell to a bunch of different companies."

"Okay," said Jerry, "in that case, you need someone in your company who fills the role of the client. The Scrum terminology for that person is called the 'Product Owner.' Sorry to be throwing jargon at you, but we have to call them something. The Product Owner owns the product, as it were. I bet you have a project manager that fills that role now, or is it your job as CTO?"

"I guess that'd be me. But how does this Product Owner fill his days? I can't imagine the developers want me to hang around the development department the whole time answering questions. My developers would kill me if I did that."

Jerry grinned, his teeth white against his tanned face. "I bet they would. After meeting you, I'm sure they would. No, seriously, the Product Owner only needs to spend ten to twenty percent of his time with the development team. But he has to *always* be available to answer questions. He stands in the critical path of product development. His absence should never cause a bottleneck, so he has to be available all the time."

"I guess I can see that." I was pretty sure there were some flaws in his theory. It felt a little too loose to me. But I thought I'd let him go on. He certainly seemed passionate about it.

"But what the Product Owner really does is prioritize the work. He's the one who decides what work needs to be done first and what the developers should concentrate on during their Sprint. To do that, he has to know a few things."

Jerry pulled back one finger. "One, he has to know what the customer needs and where the most value is. Two"—another finger back—"he has to know about the market, what the competition is doing." Another finger. "Three, he has to know what kinds of information developers need, and in what order they need it to deliver software." His pinky didn't straighten all the way—maybe an old football injury. "Four, he has to have the skill to coordinate and prioritize the various stakeholder interests. He has to align all these interests to arrive at the highest value for everyone. Not an easy job."

"Okay, so then he sets the priorities?" I asked.

"Exactly. What he does is…well he puts together a list. At the top of the list is the stuff that is most important. In Scrum we call that list the product backlog. In it, the Product Owner describes what the product should do. And the thing that is the most important is at the top of the list, then the second most important, and so on. This means that every two weeks, or monthly, you will get *real* value delivered. In small steps, maybe, but it will get delivered."

"So the Product Owner just says to the team of developers, "Okay, during this Sprint you'll develop *this*, and then the next one *that*?"

"No."

"No? But I thought you said that he set the priorities?"

"He does. But once he's set them, it's up to the team to decide what they pull from the backlog—what they can accomplish in each Sprint. They make an estimate: okay, this is how much work each of these items will take. Given that we have six developers and four weeks, we think we can do items 1 and 2 and 3 this Sprint, but number 4 will have to wait. After a few rounds of this they get pretty good at setting what we like to call the Sprint backlog."

"Okay." I said, "They figure out exactly how much they can do, but what if something comes up? A customer needs a fix, or marketing promised something without telling anyone? Wouldn't the Product Owner have to go in and change stuff around, thus messing up all the estimates?"

"You can't."

"I can't?"

"Nope. During a Sprint you aren't allowed to make any fundamental changes. In Scrum, before each Sprint your development team is *fully flexible* regarding the work they will do in the following Sprint. But this can only succeed if the team is allowed to be *completely inflexible* on work during the current Sprint. However, that work will be completely finished by the end of the Sprint. That's why the short iterations are beneficial; after all, everything is open for discussion for the next Sprint. If it starts in two weeks, anything can be changed before then."

I held up my hands. "Whoa! This is just a little much all at once—Backlogs and Product Owners and Sprints. I'm really beat. It's been a rough day. Yesterday, I was in Washington, but that feels like it was a week ago."

Jerry smiled and stood up. "Think about it. I'm going to be in DC next week anyway. Why don't we meet for dinner or something and talk some more?"

"Sure, sounds great." We exchanged cards.

The elevator upstairs was done in one of those dark woods that screams 'British'. I looked at my reflection in the mirror. I looked terrible. This had not been a good day. I shook my head. This Scrum stuff sounded interesting in conversation at a bar, but it would introduce too much uncertainty into our product development. *We can't risk it. I'd have to have Rick reorganize the whole schedule—a schedule that's already tight. We have to get this right. We have to deliver in three months.*

The elevator dinged open. I walked down the green carpet fumbling for my room key in my pocket. *But what if we can't deliver?* I thought. My stomach tightened again. What we had been doing got us into this mess. Did I really think the same methods could get us out of it?

I opened the door and immediately headed for the bed. Maybe another talk with Jerry would be a good idea. *Keep my options open,* I thought. *I may have to do something drastic. Outsource or something. Or Scrum, or something! We have to do something. If I don't get this delivered, I'm done.*

I was asleep before my head hit the pillow.

the**essentials**

1

Embrace change. Always make changes based on new insights.

2

Feedback is essential for making a good product.

3

Scrum lets you develop in short cycles. Each cycle is called a "Sprint."

4

Scrum supports a development team by becoming *completely flexible* regarding the work in the next Sprint. In return the team needs to be *completely inflexible* regarding the work in the current Sprint, thus guaranteeing that they complete each Sprint.

5

If something is hard, do it often. That's the only way to get good at it.

6

The advantage of a fixed and short-cyclical rhythm is that you start to learn how much work you can handle in a single Sprint. You become better at estimating and thus better at making promises you can keep.

7

Only detail those things that you know your customer needs, and that add the most value. These are the things that you will deliver first.

8

It is the customer's responsibility to make the developers understand what is needed. That requires frequent and intense contact. If a customer is not willing to make such an investment, then the project apparently does not add enough value for them to take it seriously.

9

The Product Owner prioritizes the work for each Sprint in collaboration with all stakeholders. She assembles a list of required capabilities called the "product backlog", which is prioritized by value of each item.

Chapter 3:
Is Scrum for Us?

...

I woke up early. It was still dark out. I turned my head on the pillow and gazed out into a barely lightening grey sky. It was still raining.

I stared at the ceiling. *This is scary*, I thought. We could lose Logistrux. In this economy that wouldn't be good. Already some of our clients had gone out of business; all of them had been forced to cut back. Logistrux was the only one who wanted something big, something new. If we could get it done, we could probably sell the same technology to everyone else. If we couldn't, we'd be dead in the water. I felt the muscles tighten one by one down my back, radiating out from my shoulders.

Okay, Mark, I asked myself, what are you going to do? I thought back to last night at the bar. Jerry was right. We needed feedback from Logistrux. Not based on documents or interviews, but based on our product. The problem was simple; we weren't ready. There were a bunch of different kinds of databases for different platforms that weren't combining accurately. And the web access: if we got it working in Internet Explorer, it looked terrible in Firefox, and worse in Chrome.

I dropped my feet over the side of the bed to the floor and stood up. I walked over to the window and looked out. *Hmm. But really that's just the last bit of work.* We had maybe eighty percent done that worked. We could show them that, couldn't we? It might gain us some credibility too—credibility that I desperately needed. Show them that we'd done a lot of work already, something I suspected they might not yet believe. I started to feel a bit better as I brushed my teeth.

What if we just took out everything that was giving us problems and gave the rest to Logistrux as a beta release?

They could give us feedback now, rather than in three months when I absolutely had to have the project completely finished. It wasn't completely like that Scrum thing Jerry was talking about, but it was an idea. And I really needed something.

I jumped in the shower. It was still early, so I bet I could catch Jerry at breakfast.

. . .

"Mark!" Jerry waved at me with the scrambled egg spoon on the buffet.

I walked up and started filling a plate besides him. "Free for breakfast?"

"As you can see, my fans follow me everywhere." He gestured at the room, empty but for us.

"So, I've been thinking," I said as I placed some bacon on my plate. "Suppose I were to release a product to one of my customers—a product with limited functionality?"

We walked toward a table and sat down as I continued, "I'd tell them it was a beta, of course, but that would be a pretty good way of getting feedback, no?"

"Hmm." He carefully buttered his toast. He spread it out with military precision: no corner of the bread escaped the butter advance. "That could be a good idea. But I wouldn't call it a beta. That sends the wrong message, both to your customer and to yourself. It says it doesn't have to be good. I'd say it was a product increment, or a 'feature set.' That way, you're saying that while it's only a part of the product, it's a part that is done. That's ready."

He bit into the toast with a look of bliss. He followed it with some scrambled eggs, then a sip of coffee, each with intentional precision. "That way your team and your customer have the right focus. Never do betas. Never do work that you don't think is good. You either give your customer something good, or you don't. There is no 'try.'"

"Yes, Yoda."

He grinned. "Okay, here's what I would do. Propose this to your customer; see if they're open to the idea. But beware the dark side. Make sure they commit to using the software. If they don't use it, you get no feedback. And no feedback doesn't mean it's good."

I watched him do the toast, scrambled egg, coffee sequence again. "But I do think," he said when he finished, "that it's a good idea. A product that you can test with limited functionality is better than no product at all. But"—he looked up sharply—"make sure it's good. Better no work than bad work!"

I sat back for a second. He was right. If you delivered something poorly made, you had to work ten times as hard to fix that first impression. "The user interfaces in particular have to be perfect." Jerry leaned forward, "If some button points to a feature that doesn't exist yet, it needs to show that very clearly if someone clicks on it. In Scrum we use a 'Definition of Done,' but I can explain that to you another time. Just make sure that every single time you deliver something to a client it fully complies with your own quality standards. That's very important. Don't scrimp on that."

That's what I was going to do. First thing Monday, I'd shut down the two problem areas, then get the testers in to test what we had. Once we'd gotten that stable…hmm, give it a month? That's when I would call Logistrux and propose a limited release.

"That sounds good, Jerry. I'm looking forward to talking to you more when you're in DC next week. I'd like to bring along Rick, one of my project managers. If we decide to go ahead with Scrum, he'd be the guy I'd want to implement it."

Toast, eggs, coffee. "That may not be the best idea."

"Why not?"

"Well, **Scrum doesn't have project managers. Instead, the team is empowered. They're responsible for the outcome, and they can manage themselves. The classic project manager 'boss' of the team isn't needed in Scrum. The team plans each Sprint based on the priorities of the Product Owner. They divide the work among themselves, make progress transpar-**

ent and monitor themselves. For most project managers, that's a hard change to make."

"Hold up. Developing software without a project manager? That's insane. You'd have a lot of chiefs and no Indians." I spread my hands. "Someone has to tell the engineers what to do; someone has to be in charge."

"Nope. You're wrong. You don't need a boss. You only think you do because you've been conditioned to think that way." Just coffee this time. He'd finished the toast. "Isn't the definition of insanity doing the same thing over and over and expecting different results?"

"What do you mean?"

"Think about it this way; what you're doing is infantilizing your software developers. They're smart workers. Once they accept responsibility, as a team, for delivering the software by a given date, they'll do it. Knowledge workers need to be facilitated, not controlled. Give them clear goals and the freedom to manage themselves, and you'll have a smooth-running machine."

I looked at him skeptically. He obviously picked up on it. "Here." He leaned forward, rested his elbows on the table. "What you need above all is a clear vision of what should be done. Then make a prioritized list of features. The team estimates the size of each feature and chooses which features they can accomplish in a Sprint."

"Then you need to establish a working rhythm for the team. **You do need someone who supports the project and makes the process run smoothly. I'll give you that. In Scrum we call this person the Scrum Master. But his job is only to manage the process, keep it running well, and make sure the rhythm is maintained. But the Scrum Master is not the boss!**"

He brought up a finger to emphasize his point. "It's more of a facilitating role—definitely not a project manager role. The job is to take the initiative and remove problems that are giving the team trouble. But that's it. The traditional project manager doesn't exist in Scrum. The Scrum Master is the oil in the process, making sure everything is running smoothly."

"Hmm. All right, let's definitely talk more next week." We were both done with breakfast and I looked at my watch; I was *not* missing another plane. Nine a.m. Still plenty of time. "Anything else I should think about before then?"

"Well, maybe," said Jerry. "Let's talk about your development environment. Mind you, Scrum is an approach that's only concerned with the *management* of software development. It's the most detailed and rigorous project management process I know of. Scrum is the only approach to project management that allows developers to estimate the work at this level of detail. And it supports them in keeping their promises. But it really doesn't say anything in particular about engineering practices."

"I have a feeling you're going to say something about them, regardless." I leaned back at this point.

"Yep. There are some good ones out there, and you might as well use them when working with Scrum. I'll give you one example: a fully automated product build process. Getting the correct version of the source code, compiling, ensuring transparency integrating, and building an installer. Completely automate that. It's too easy to make mistakes and lose time if you're doing it by hand."

True enough, I thought.

"After you've done that, after it's built, you always, always, have to run a comprehensive automated test. If it passes that test, you at least have some assurance of quality. And if everything is still working since the last build, that's good to know. An automated build and test environment is really required at this point. If you don't already have that, you have to move on this immediately."

Jerry smiled, then drank some more coffee and frowned slightly at its coolness. "Anyway, here's how that ties into Scrum. If you want to incrementally deliver a product every two weeks or once a month, you have to prove that it still works each and every time. You can't be delivering bad product. And if you have to test your product fully every two weeks or so, your testing will get more and more involved with every Sprint as the product gets bigger and bigger. You could continually hire new testers, I suppose," he chuckled, "but automating your testing seems like a cheaper option. And it makes you constantly aware of the quality of your whole product."

It hit me then. "You're totally right!" I blurted out.

"I often am."

"No, I'm serious. During our last release the guy who always puts the finishing touches on before we burn the disks was out with a broken leg. We messed up some transparency issues and had to throw away the first shipment of DVD's. Total pain in the ass. So we dramatically improved our build system. Not at the point of pushing of one button at the moment, but we're getting there. That we could do in a couple days."

"Mmm hmm." Coffee again. The waitress had been by to warm it up.

"The test environment. That may take a bit longer. I know some of the testers have something running, but not complete. Hmm. Maybe it would make sense if we developed automated tests as we built each new part of the software. The developers are already writing that part; wouldn't be hard to write tests as well. We take those, put them in the test environment, and bang, we can prove quality for every new build."

"Nice thinking. We call that test-driven development. Again, not really part of Scrum, but it really helps. Anyway, I gotta go catch my flight."

I glanced at my watch. "Yeah, me too. Missing another one is just not an option."

. . .

I managed to sleep most of the flight back. Anne picked me up at Dulles, as she always liked to after a trip. We got a good forty minutes to talk alone before anything could intrude.

"How was it?" she asked. Her eyes concentrated on the road ahead.

"Bad." I stared at the light Saturday traffic. "Really bad."

"I'm so sorry. Was it as bad as you were afraid of? Did they pull out?" She glanced at me quickly. She knew the score. If our biggest client, who was paying for all our development, pulled out because of something my team couldn't deliver—well, they'd have to blame someone, and the logical person would be me. This was not a good time to be looking for a job.

"Not yet." I exhaled heavily. "I got three more months."

"Before you left, you told me you needed at least six."

"I know."

"What are you going to do?"

"Well," I told her, "Maybe something crazy. You see, I met this guy…"

. . .

I was still jetlagged when I hit the office on Monday. Too many time zones too fast—and the anxiety didn't help. I was at the office before seven a.m. The place was just about empty. I wandered through the maze of cubicles. They were that odd greenish, greyish brown that only industrial furniture designers thought wouldn't drain the souls of everyone who worked in them.

Most people, as people do everywhere, had put up pictures of their family, or maybe their wedding. I had managed to relax a bit on Sunday with Anne, but now, looking at these empty cubicles, I thought about how these people were counting on me. Even the pictures might be gone if we didn't pull a rabbit out of the hat.

I turned into the testing area, and there was George. He was a couple of years out of Carnegie Mellon young, nice, and personable. He was good with users, and knew the product inside and out.

"Hey boss," he said as he swiveled around. He had mutton-chop whiskers, which I guessed was either a hipster thing or a sign that he was into civil war re- enactments. I'd never asked which—embarrassed to show my ignorance, I guess. I tried to picture him in a Confederate uniform and couldn't quite get his pear-shaped body into the gray. "How was London?"

"Shitty weather. Chilly reception. No fun, to be honest. Next time Logistrux is pissed, you get to go."

Jeff Sutherland, Rini van Solingen, Eelco Rustenburg

"No thanks! I'm far happier here." He smiled. "Hey, can I bring something up? I think we may have a problem."

"Sure thing." I leaned against a nearby desk, folding my arms. "Shoot."

"I've looked at the new plan from Rick, and it only gives us two weeks to test. That's just crazy. We need at least six weeks. We've got to test, and then we've got to fix all the bugs we find. We can't do it in two weeks. But Rick said given the deadline, we just don't have the time."

"Let me talk with him about it. Maybe we can work something out," I said. "I've got something for you too."

"You do?" George sounded surprised.

"I want you to set up a test environment that we can run after each build. And it has to be automated."

He cocked his head. "An automated regression test? Or more than that?"

"More." I replied. "I want there to be a functional regression test in it, but I want the developers to be able to upload their automated test too. The idea is that we eventually want a comprehensive automatic testing script we can run after each build. I want to be able to push one button and have the complete product built and tested using a full system test."

"That would be awesome! I've been playing around with something like that already. I already automate my own testing—saves a ton of time. If it doesn't pass the automated test, there's no reason to go any further. Let me see if I can expand on it. I'll sit down with Susan this afternoon and see if it'll work for the developers too."

Susan was one of our senior developers. She was always open to trying something new, but incredibly pragmatic about it at the same time. Definitely the right choice. I looked at George with a new eye. "Good call. Let me know if it's feasible by, say, Wednesday?"

"Yeah. I think that would work."

"Good. Well, back to the mine."

I turned and walked through the empty cubes again. Well, that was one thing moved on. I looked at a calendar on someone's desk. It was the 21st. We now had three days less than three months.

I sat down at my desk and found an email from Jerry in my inbox. He would get in Tuesday and be in DC till Saturday. He suggested dinner Thursday night and a visit to our office on Friday. Thursday worked, but I was booked almost solid on Friday.

I decided he could spend the afternoon with Rick, and see if the two of them could come up with some ways to accelerate the project. Friday would be the 25th. A week of our three months would be gone.

I sent Rick a meeting request. I sent another to George asking him to demo the product for a West Coast visitor. Almost an instantaneous yes from both of them. Rick must have been driving and emailing again. That was going to get him killed one day.

Jeff Sutherland, Rini van Solingen, Eelco Rustenburg

the**essentials**

1

Scrum works with cycles of a fixed length called a "Sprint." Sprints last from one to four weeks. At the end of a Sprint, the team delivers a releasable product.

2

Using Scrum, the product is *always* ready. You are able to deliver a version of your product that is at most one Sprint old.

3

A Scrum team should be seven people plus or minus two.

4

A Sprint opens with a presentation of the work for that Sprint called the "Sprint backlog." The team asks questions to clarify exactly what is expected.

5

In the Sprint planning meeting, items on the Sprint backlog are split into individual tasks. These tasks should take between 2 and 4 hours of work, with a maximum of 2 days.

6

The team subdivides the work and delivers a realistic plan to which the team must give an explicit commitment.

7

The Scrum Master ensures that daily stand-ups are held at a fixed time every day for up to 15 minutes. During the daily stand-up, everyone answers only three questions: 1. What have you done since yesterday? 2. What will you do today? 3. What is keeping you from doing stuff?

8

The goal of the stand-up is to ensure that the team has the best and most productive day possible.

9

Impediments are road-blocks that prevent a team from completing the Sprint. The Scrum Master takes responsibility for resolving them.

Chapter 4:
The Scrum Process

...

Jerry and I met at Central, downtown. It was one of my favorite restaurants, and Jerry's too, it turned out. He had lived here for eight years before moving back to San Francisco a few years back. His daughter was six, and she lived here with her mother. They'd been divorced about three years. He flew in just about every other weekend. It was tiring, he told me, but worth it to see his little girl—and he could usually combine the trips with business. This week he had given a two-day Certified Scrum Master course in Baltimore. I could tell that if I offered him a longer contract, he'd jump at it.

"You look worried," said Jerry.

"I am. It's the 24th. I have less than three months now to deliver this project. I've been thinking about our conversation in London. I'm impressed with your insight. I'm not so sure about Scrum, but we have to do something drastic." I put my hands flat on the table. "We're up against the wall here, Jerry."

"Okay, tell me what you've done since you got back in the office."

I told him about George's automated testing. He and Susan had presented a model of it to me yesterday. They'd put some time in and linked the automated testing to the build process. It looked like it would work. It wasn't complete yet, but it would save time. There were still only a limited number of tests in the system, I told Jerry, so we still needed to work on that. But once we were up and running, we'd be doing the automatic build and test every night. Every morning we would know what bugs we had created the day before and could fix them. Already that was a big improvement.

"Sounds like you're already taking some action," said Jerry.

"I'm trying," I said as we both perused the menu. He ordered the scallops; I went with the steak au poivre.

After the waitress took our order, I looked across at Jerry. "So, I'm interested in Scrum. But I'm a little unsure about the whole thing. It seems so undefined, like the product is never done."

"Let me turn that around on you," said Jerry. **"You say it's never finished. I say it's *always* finished. Each Sprint you have a new, stable product. If your Sprint is two weeks, then every two weeks your product is done. It's also a maximum of two weeks old, so you're always ready!** I doubt you can do that now. I bet you can't even ship your product. When was the last time you put out a release? I'm betting at least six months."

"A year. The latest stable version of our product that I can ship to customers is a year old. There's a lot of demand for new functions. They're functions we've already developed, but I can't release them because it's just not stable."

"And?"

"All right, let's try this. I'm still not totally sold on Scrum, but the only certainty I have right now is of failure. Let's do a pilot project. We'll see if it delivers what you're promising, and whether our developers like it. Why don't you come on board for three months and we can re-evaluate then."

"Okay," said Jerry. "One thing, though."

"What?"

"I expect Scrum will work well for you. However," he raised one finger, "It's not up to you to decide whether to work with Scrum; it's up to the developers themselves."

"I'm sorry," I said. "They work for me."

Jerry steepled his fingers. "Yes, Mark, you are the boss. But you're not the boss of your developer's working processes. One of the principles of Scrum is that the development team manages themselves. They alone are the masters of their own processes and tools. *What* is developed using those processes and tools is determined by the Product Owner. *How* it is developed is decided by the team."

The food arrived and conversation stopped for a few moments. After a few bites I was going to start arguing, but Jerry leapt in first.

"Let me put it this way. What's the worst part of your job?"

"Well, budgets are no fun..."

"Stop! You're lying—a polite lie, but a lie nonetheless. The worst part of your job is managing all these smart, stubborn, pain-in-the-ass developers. Admit it!"

I raised my hands, acknowledging defeat. "You got me. You got me."

"And the fun part about being a CTO is being an inspirational leader, providing strategy, vision, seeing a better future and aiming your people at it! That's the fun part. Your responsibility is to make clear to the team that they should be in control of their own work processes, and show them how to do that."

"So I shouldn't just tell them we're switching to Scrum?"

"C'mon, Mark," he said, "how well will that work? You know as well as I that if the team really doesn't want to use a methodology, it won't work. Let them make their own assessment. Scrum works. It is designed to make them faster, better, stronger than they were before!"

I widened my eyes in mock wonder. "You did not just say that."

"I did. Hyperbole aside, I'm serious. Explain the process to them. Tell them why it's important to the company's goals. But ultimately the team decides. If they aren't committed, it won't work anyway. They have to be engaged, and that's a personal decision."

"True enough. I don't even want to tell you how many 'smarter, better' flavors of the month I've had shoved down my throat in my career. But that's why I still have a few doubts about Scrum. Before I ask the team to do it, I need to be convinced." I took a quick bite. Delicious.

"Go on. What questions do you have?" asked Jerry.

"All right. This self-management, how does it actually work? I don't want the team constantly discussing how to tackle a problem. I want them to tackle the problem. That's the role of project managers: to get them pointed in the right direction."

"Okay." Jerry said. "Let me explain. **The work in a Sprint is disciplined and well defined. Everyone knows what is expected from them, and when. Self-management by the team is pretty much built into the Scrum process itself. The times for discussion are scheduled up front. Outside of those limited occasions, people will be working on product development only.**"

"Okay." I said a touch skeptically.

"Also," Jerry paused for a second for a sip of wine. "Scrum works best within small teams. The rule of thumb is seven people, plus or minus two. Keeping the team small keeps the lines of communication short, and, ideally, lets you put them all in the same room. And remember the Scrum Master? I'll get into this more later, but he acts as a facilitator, making sure the team doesn't block itself."

We both turned to our food for a minute. Then Jerry waved his fork. "So, remember how the Product Owner presents the work that needs to be done? He breaks it all down into work items, often in the form of what we call 'user stories.' We want to see the system from the user's perspective to give him a better working experience with the software. The team needs to work with the Product Owner regularly to help build out the stories, break them down into smaller stories, and roughly estimate how long they'll take at a high level before they are ready to be worked on."

"So each Sprint begins with each team reviewing stories that are in a ready state and asking the Product Owner questions until they have a very clear idea of what needs to be done. That may take an hour or two. After that, the team knows exactly what is expected of them in the next few weeks. Then they plan the work themselves, during what we call a Sprint planning meeting, by breaking down all those stories into individual tasks."

"How broad are those tasks?" I asked.

"You want them to be pretty small, something you can finish in a few hours. If a task is going to take a couple of days, it's too big; break it into smaller sub-tasks. You also, ideally, want a single developer to be able to complete the task. So if you have a two-day, two-developer task, you break it up. If it's too hard to break up, that usually indicates that what needs to be done is not clear enough, or it's not clear enough what the end result should be. You don't include those in a Sprint; it'll waste too much time. When they've become clear, you can put them in a Sprint."

"Isn't that just kicking the problem down the road?"

"Oh, you should look into it, research it, and in extreme cases, bring it in, but timebox it—set a predefined length of time you're going to work on it. Then put it into the next Sprint. It's a sign that someone hasn't thought something through. If the user experience is not clear, it will take at least twice as much work to get that task done. It doesn't make sense to waste the team's time like this."

"Okay."

"Man, these are good scallops." Jerry took another bite, savoring it. "Okay, so you have everything broken down into tasks. You know how long each one will take. You know how many engineers you have. You do the math. After the Sprint planning meeting, the feasibility of the Sprint becomes clear. If all the work won't fit into the Sprint, the team works with the Product Owner to see which items need to be moved to the next Sprint. If it looks like they'll be able to do more, then it's decided what can be added to the Sprint."

I hesitated for a second; then, memories of day-long meetings rising to the fore, I said, "How long do these last? Doesn't that waste the time of the whole team? Usually I just have Rick figure all that out so the team can focus on their work."

"Oh, it's not bad—couple of hours," Jerry replied. "It varies based on the length of the Sprint, the quality of the backlog and the experience of the team, but usually never more than half a day. Now I know you're saying that's a lot of time for the whole team to be unproductive, but there's a lot that happens in those meetings. The team discusses dependencies, estimates how long things will take, reflects on problems and possible solutions, coordinates who needs to be involved, and so on. That can't all be done just by Rick sitting in an office by himself. This is when the whole team becomes invested, involved—they become *aligned*. I bet Rick has to talk to them anyway; he just does it without any plan."

I stopped eating. "You know, you're right. I've had some developers complain that Rick interrupts them a lot. It's not the questions, it's the timing. They're right in the middle of something when he bugs them. Rick has started to schedule meetings with them each week."

Jerry nodded. "The most important thing about the Sprint planning meeting is that the team picks the amount of work they think is doable. No team will work according to a plan they think is impossible. If it can't be done, why do it? Then, once everyone agrees there's a viable plan, everyone commits to carrying it out. Everyone, as a team - not as individuals - but as a team. They say, 'We, collectively, are responsible for completing the Sprint.'"

"Let me make sure I understand you," I said with a certain amount of skepticism. "Within half a day, the whole team knows what they are going to do, how they are going to go about it, and how long it will take. And then they all commit to that as a team. Sounds a little 'kumbaya' to me."

"All right," said Jerry, with only slight exasperation in his voice. "All right, how long does it take you to put together your plans now? And just as importantly, how much fun do your developers have in the process?"

"Fun?"

"Yeah, fun."

"Well, fun doesn't really enter into it."

"Why not?"

"Well, you're right, it can take a while. Rick has to go to a bunch of different people, get all their input. Then he comes up with a plan, a plan most people are agreed on. There are always a few holdouts. You know how it is—some people think it can be done, some think it's not feasible technically. And sometimes they're right; things don't work the way we thought. But re-doing the plan takes a long time."

"And so you keep going with a plan that you know is wrong?"

"Well, everyone knows Rick is working on a new one."

Jerry looked at me levelly. "Let me get this straight. Your planning process takes so long that it's better to work according to a plan that you know is outdated, a plan you know will only lead to failure. And you expect your people to be excited about that? To be committed to that?"

"Well..."

"Come on Mark, listen to yourself."

"Okay, Jerry." I could hear myself getting defensive. "Are you saying that with Scrum the plans never go wrong? I can't believe that's possible; there are always things you don't anticipate."

Jerry smiled. An odd, kindly smile, as if he'd seen my defensiveness a thousand times before. "Of course, Mark," he said gently. "In Scrum, like in anything else, planning doesn't always go smoothly. It's hard at first. But doing hard things over and over is the only way to get better at them. Plus, let's say you totally get it wrong. You've only wasted two weeks; you can course correct at the next planning meeting."

"So Scrum doesn't magically make all your problems go away? That's what it sounds like you've been saying."

"No. Scrum doesn't solve your problems; it just makes them painfully visible." He laughed. "Scrum is just like your mother-in-law: always pointing out all those things not being done right, and not doing anything herself!"

I laughed along with him. It was getting late. I offered to walk him back to his hotel. He talked about his daughter; I talked about Anne. I asked him if I could pick his brain for just a few more minutes.

· · ·

We came in through the grand entrance of the Willard, grabbed a seat at one of the elegant couches lining the wide passageway, waved down a waiter, and ordered espresso.

"Okay," I said. "What happens next? They've got a plan, then what?"

"Well," Jerry replied, "if they've broken everything down into stories and those stories into tasks, and they've selected the tasks that can fit within the Sprint, and everyone is committed, the Sprint begins. In less than a day, everyone knows what they have to do, and they can all get to work."

"But you said they manage themselves. I have to say, I'm struggling with that one. How do things run while they're working? Who monitors their progress?"

"Listen, Mark, you make the whole process transparent. Honest. Anyone can monitor progress. But the best thing is to have the team do it. They're responsible for it. After a two-week Sprint it will become obvious pretty quickly if they're not getting their work done. Then you can talk with them about how to improve. During the Sprint itself we have the Scrum Master. You remember that role?"

"Yeah, I think so."

"I'll break it down into basic steps. Every day the Scrum Master holds a meeting, usually called the 'daily stand-up' or Scrum meeting. It's at the same time every day, and it lasts no more than fifteen minutes."

I must have looked surprised because he quickly clarified. "The meeting is tightly focused. Everyone stands up, no sitting; this is an active meeting. No doodling, no staring off into space, no endless PowerPoint presentations. No, this meeting is when the team coordinates their work; everyone has to be present."

"All right."

"Seriously, Mark, you sit people down at a table, give them a pad, a cup of coffee, they're protected, they're safe. Making them stand up and take ownership is much more open and active. And"—Jerry grinned at me—"it takes less time!"

I arched my eyebrows.

"It works. People aren't allowed to lean against the wall. If someone's late, there's usually some form of punishment; doing push-ups, or having to get coffee for everybody, ten bucks in the pot, whatever. The point is you have to be active, aware, and on time. This is a meeting everyone has to take seriously. And, as it's only fifteen minutes, there is no excuse."

"When do you do it?" I asked. "First thing in the morning?"

"That's typical, though I've also seen people do it right before lunch. Haven't seen it at the end of the day; doesn't mean it wouldn't work, though."

"Okay, fifteen minutes. What can you accomplish in that amount of time?"

Our espresso arrived. We both sipped appreciatively.

Jerry set his cup down on the saucer. "You're right; you can only accomplish a few things in fifteen minutes, so it's really simple. **The stand-up has only one very clear goal. How can we have the best and most effective day possible as a team? To do that people are only asked three questions. One: what have you done since the last stand-up? Two: what will you achieve before the next stand-up? And three: what's getting in your way?"**

Jerry raised his fingers one at a time in swift, emphatic motions, moving his whole arm. "The first question is about results accomplished: what did you work on yesterday that will help the team meet the Sprint goal, and what was the result? The second addresses the future: how are you going to help the team move forward the next day? And the third is asked to see if you've had any insights into problems that might lead to the Sprint failing. What's keeping you from doing your work? It's all about how to make the team successful— sort of like a rugby scrum, except the game is more complicated and takes longer."

"That could be really helpful." I said as I sipped my espresso. I loved the Willard's espresso; it was better than Starbucks any day. "I'm often amazed that developers don't communicate with each other. And there are so many interdependencies that they could help each other with, especially that third question. I can't tell you how many times I've found out that different developers are spending time to fix the same problem—almost always in incompatible ways."

"Exactly," said Jerry. "And these stand-ups force them to communicate. It's not that they don't want to; it's just that they don't have a forum to do it, and they aren't required to do it. The stand-ups set a rhythm of sharing their progress and their problems. With new teams, there can be some discomfort at first, and that's where Scrum Masters earn their money. The idea is that they make sure the team is energetic, honest, and open during these meetings, that one person doesn't dominate or lecture, or another person doesn't withdraw."

"And here's the best part." Jerry paused for effect. I could tell he enjoyed a little dramatic tension as he leaned in a bit. "The best part is, everyone will manage their time better. They've personally made a promise to the team to get something done before the next day. It makes them far more task-oriented. And then they actually learn just how much they can accomplish in a single day of work. Maybe for the first time, everyone will focus on being effective each and every day."

"Really?" I asked. "How so?"

"Think about it. You come to the meeting three days in a row with only vague progress to show for it. How are you going to feel? You're breaking your word to your teammates. That doesn't feel good. You'll get better."

"All right, so what about the problems?" I asked. "You aren't going to fix problems in fifteen minutes—I don't care how task-oriented you are."

"You're right; that's not what the stand-ups are for. They're to point out problems—or what in Scrum we call 'impediments'. **Impediments are roadblocks that prevent the achievement of what you want to accomplish: completing the Sprint. When developers have to report them every single day, they can be addressed right away.**"

"By who? When?" This still seemed a bit vague to me.

"This is the other part of the Scrum Master's job. He'll ask people with impediments to stay a bit longer to work on them. No need to take up the whole team's time. Most of the time, they can be handled within the team, by redistributing work or making sure a couple of developers work together. But sometimes they have to be brought to the Product Owner. He might re-prioritize tasks, or split them up. Maybe it's just a case of buying new servers or getting a new library, or getting some time from a DBA. The key point, though, is to synchronize as a team, even for those impediments that are outside the team's control. Sometimes it's more important to determine who *isn't* going to do anything about a problem, so they can go focus on something else instead of banging their heads against a brick wall that they can't do anything about."

"But isn't that disheartening?"

"Here's how it works in practice. If there's a problem the team can't handle, the Scrum Master takes it up, and figures out who or what can make that problem go away. He's the one responsible for removing impediments. It's not that he is actually the one doing it; he's just the one making sure it happens. The important thing—and this is why it not only *isn't* disheartening, but can actually be empowering—is that impediments are handled quickly! In one day! The rule is that an impediment is resolved before the next stand-up, within a single day. An impediment puts the whole Sprint at risk, so it has to be taken seriously."

"Really?" I ask. "Not all problems can be solved that quickly."

"They can if they're important." Jerry set down his empty espresso cup. "And the Scrum Master is held accountable by the same process as the team. He has to answer the same three questions the team does: he also has to say what he's done since the last standup."

"I've gotta get going," I said, standing. "It's after midnight. My wife is going to kill me. I'll see you tomorrow."

"See you tomorrow, Mark." We shook hands and I drove into the night. At least there wasn't much traffic.

Until I hit the beltway, of course. Where were these people going at midnight?

I drummed my fingers on the steering wheel. Let's see. The development team manages itself, schedules itself, coordinates daily progress and problems, and does it in a nice, predictable rhythm. The team chooses the best approach to achieve, in short cycles, a working project. Being in charge of themselves makes it more fun for the team. The only changes made to the product are those that add value to the customer. And the customer is highly involved; they help decide those values and they can shift them because they can give early feedback.

. . .

Anne was still up when I got home. She eyed me as I came into the kitchen.

"Coffee! Honestly, we were just talking. I was good."

"You seem a bit more relaxed."

"Well, I'm a bit more hopeful. This Scrum stuff might be able to help. I think. I'm not sure if it will actually work, much less work for us, but maybe…well, maybe. I think it will at least help us address some of our immediate problems."

She touched my shoulder, "Logistrux?"

"I don't know. I think so. I think we'll be able to give them something that works and get their feedback on it. That should help. I hope."

We moved into the bedroom. As I washed my face she asked me the question I was afraid of asking myself. "Do you think Logistrux is just playing you? Giving you enough rope to hang yourself?"

I looked at my face in the mirror. Water dripped like tears down my cheeks. The drops lingered hesitantly at my jaw line, and trembled there for a moment before leaping into the sink.

"I hope not. I don't think so. They've got too much sunk into this. I'm sure they want us to succeed. I just don't think they think we can do it. I do. But they don't trust me anymore. I keep lying to them."

"What happens if you can't keep your word this time?"

I got into bed next to her and stared at the ceiling in the dark. "Nothing good. If someone at the company can convince them to stay, it won't be with me in the mix, and if they leave….Well, you don't need the guy who couldn't deliver for the biggest client around anymore."

Her hand slipped into mine. I squeezed. "I think this Scrum stuff might just work. I'm introducing Jerry to the team tomorrow. Maybe they'll agree."

We lay there in the dark, silent. I listened as her breathing became regular, adrift in sleep. I looked up. Shadows from the lights of passing cars moved across the ceiling, starting small, then stretching across the room as if they were reaching for some sort of escape. Then they would snap back, right to the way they had been before. I spent far too long embracing that metaphor as symbolic of my whole existence before finally falling asleep.

theessentials

1

Scrum works with cycles of a fixed length called a "Sprint." Sprints last from one to four weeks. At the end of a Sprint, the team delivers a releasable product.

2

Using Scrum, the product is *always* ready. You are able to deliver a version of your product that is at most one Sprint old.

3

A Scrum team should be seven people plus or minus two.

4

A Sprint opens with a presentation of the work for that Sprint called the "Sprint backlog." The team asks questions to clarify exactly what is expected.

5

In the Sprint planning meeting, items on the Sprint backlog are split into individual tasks. These tasks should take between 2 and 4 hours of work, with a maximum of 2 days.

6

The team subdivides the work and delivers a realistic plan to which the team must give an explicit commitment.

7

The Scrum Master ensures that daily stand-ups are held at a fixed time every day for up to 15 minutes. During the daily stand-up, everyone answers only three questions: 1. What have you done since yesterday? 2. What will you do today? 3. What is keeping you from doing stuff?

8

The goal of the stand-up is to ensure that the team has the best and most productive day possible.

9

Impediments are road blocks that prevent a team from completing the Sprint. The Scrum Master takes responsibility for resolving them.

Chapter 5:
Shall We Try It?

...

I was at the office early again. I hadn't slept well and figured I might as well be there. Jerry was coming in later, so I figured I'd shoot off a few emails early to clear that part of my day. The parking lot was empty when I pulled in. I parked and got out of the car. God, I was exhausted. I sat at my desk and stared straight ahead for a few moments…or minutes…I lost track of the time. I didn't really think of anything. I just sat there. Not gathering myself, exactly. Emptying myself. I was the leader of this team. They had faith in me. I had to let go of the worry. Let go of the fear. I could curl up and cry at home. Not here.

I blinked a few times and rose to face the day.

...

Jerry walked into the lobby right at one o'clock. We headed upstairs. I walked him through the space, poured him a cup of coffee, and headed for my office. Rick was already there.

"Nice to meet you, Jerry. Rick." Rick extended his thick hand. I hadn't briefed him too much, just told him to read up a bit on Scrum.

"I'm George," said George. He was there to give a full demo. I thought Jerry should understand exactly what we did.

After a few minutes of small talk, the demo started. Jerry had good, insightful questions. We went back and forth for a bit. By around two o'clock I thought he had a good grasp of the product, and changed the conversation.

"Okay. That's the product. You know about the problems we're having with Logistrux. And everyone here knows just how serious they are." I made eye contact with Rick and George. Rick nodded. He'd been around the block. He knew the stakes. George blinked and swallowed. I stared at him for a moment. He needed to realize exactly what was happening.

"I think Jerry has some ideas that might be able to help us. So I thought I'd get him here to talk about it. Jerry, where do we start?"

"Well, I want to get some fine detail on the issues you're having. I'll be giving a talk on Scrum to the full team in a bit, so let me take some time getting an idea of what the roadblocks are."

"Fair enough. Rick?"

Rick began to summarize the last year. He was a little defensive of his team. "They've worked their butts off," he said. "There were no clear requirements at the beginning of the project, but they all started to work on that themselves. Logistrux had a big idea, but the team actually wrote up the requirements it implied. They did ask Logistrux to take a look at them when they finished, but Logistrux didn't really say much. So we thought we were in good shape."

"But you weren't," said Jerry.

No, Rick admitted. They hadn't been. Once they'd started to actually make the software, Logistrux just kept requesting change after change. Rick blamed the delays on Logistrux.

"It's their fault," his voice was beginning to rise. "They kept on changing the requirements. Of course things were going to slip. You can't just turn on a dime. One time we had to throw whole sections of the software away because they'd changed their minds. My team did a good job, dammit!"

I started to say something but Jerry raised his hand and leaned forward.

"Let's start from where we are now."

Rick took a big breath. He let it out. "Okay."

"Are the requirements stable now?"

"Well, for us they are," Rick said. "I mean, it's a lot clearer what we need to build. We know what we're incorporating into the product. But whether that's *precisely* what Logistrux needs is something I just don't know. Logistrux, as big as they are, aren't our only customers;

we have to take into account a lot more functionality than just what Logistrux needs."

Jerry steepled his fingers in front of his face. "Explain that to me."

"Okay. So a lot of different people use the product. Each of them has their own environment that we have to be sensitive to. Just one example: which web browser do they use? We've got it working in Internet Explorer, but we can't just release that. We have to make sure it works in Chrome and Safari and Firefox. Heck, I bet someone is still using Netscape for some godforsaken reason. We get it working in one, it looks terrible in another. Complete nightmare."

I was surprised; this was news to me. I had thought that we couldn't connect to the web and display well at all. I had had no idea that Internet Explorer was working well. I decided not to bring it up at the moment, but I thought we could certainly do a pre-release for Logistrux. That would buy us something, no? And we'd get better feedback. I stood up, and I realized I felt a bit better. I'd made a decision. Better something than nothing.

"Before we continue further, let's have Jerry present to the group. I've asked everyone to gather in the auditorium to hear what Jerry has to say."

Rick stood up and looked at me. He knew that something had just changed; he just didn't know what. "Sounds good."

• • •

There were about a hundred developers and testers in the room. They quieted down after I took the podium.

"I'm sure you've all heard by now that Logistrux is not happy with us." The room went quiet. I wasn't usually this direct with bad news. "The rumors are right. They're not happy with us at all."

I looked out at them. I had their attention now. "We have to make changes. If we continue as we are...well, that isn't an option anymore. That's been taken away from us. Anyway, I invited Jerry here to talk to us about Scrum. But let me make something clear: I'm not going to impose

Scrum on you guys. I do want your opinions, though. I think it might help. Let me know what you think."

I stood aside and let Jerry take center stage. I was trying to keep Jerry's dictates in mind. Scrum wouldn't only be a change in our process, but a change in the very philosophy of managing developers. I hoped Jerry could sell them on it.

Jerry began to talk. **"Scrum is a change of culture. This isn't just a change in how you do things. It's a change of culture itself. The team gains enormous responsibility, but also enormous authority. But you don't have to wait to change. You can start right away. You only have to change the way you look at things—your mindset."**

Jerry sold it—a real performance. There was knowing laughter as he described things that could go wrong in practice, some of which seemed eerily similar to things we'd run into.

He then went to the fundamental insight behind Scrum, and behind 'Agile.' He put up a slide with the **Agile Manifesto:**

"We are uncovering better ways of developing software by doing it and helping others do it. Through this work we have come to value:

> *Individuals and interactions* over processes and tools.
> *Working software* over comprehensive documentation.
> *Customer collaboration* over contract negotiation.
> *Responding to change* over following a plan.

That is, while there is value on the items on the right, we value the items on the left more."

I looked at the slide for a moment and thought about it. There was some truth to it. I was a 'deal is a deal' kind of person. There's a procedure; you have to follow it. But at the same time, I often found it infuriating when people blindly followed procedures without thinking, even ones that I had created. As I thought more about it I realized that fundamentally I believed that the product, and the quality of that product, was the most important thing. Process should always take a back seat. I'd never quite put it that way before, but I knew I believed it.

Documentation? Man, what a pain to do, but I hated "cowboy" programmers who never did any. Transferring their work to anyone else could be almost impossible. I always stressed to my teams that everything had to be documented. But when I actually used software, I never looked at the documentation at first. If I had to, I cursed the programmers for not making it intuitive and easy; that was their job. Good software, I realized, shouldn't need comprehensive documentation.

I looked at the other principles and found myself nodding in agreement. I also realized that believing something in principle isn't the same as putting it into practice, and that I often didn't. I almost grinned. Doing the right thing is sometimes hard.

I realized I'd missed a few minutes of Jerry's talk while sunk in my thoughts. He'd moved on to the standard approach to requirements: requiring them all up front. He called that approach "frozen."

"So, let's just lay out some of the assumptions inherent in that, okay?" Jerry walked back and forth in front of the audience. "This assumes that you as a customer, and you as a team, have had the best ideas up front—before the project starts. Do you honestly believe that you aren't going to have better ideas later on? I certainly hope not. That would imply that you simply stopped thinking when you started writing code!"

He stopped for a second. "So you have your 'perfect' requirements that aren't going to change, no matter what. What happens next? You come up with a budget—how much money this is going to cost; and a plan—how long it's going to take. But really, you're smart people; you *know* that those aren't going to be perfect. And you *know* that your list of requirements isn't perfect either. Think about that. You're basing your professional life on a lie! A lie you're telling yourself! And you're surprised when you run into reality and find out you've been lying this whole time!"

"Here's what happens." Jerry lowered his voice. "Here's what happens. During the project you start to negotiate tradeoffs between money and time. Everything becomes negotiable. Things aren't delivered on time. They cost more than they should. And then you make the fatal mistake: you make quality negotiable too. Once you start negotiating quality…" He trailed off.

"It's like that old apocryphal story about Churchill where he runs into this lady at a party, and says, 'Madam, would you sleep with me for five million pounds?' And she's all flustered and says, 'My goodness, Mr. Churchill… Well, I suppose… we would have to discuss terms, of course…' And then Churchill bursts in, 'Would you sleep with me for five pounds?' And she gets all indignant: 'Mr. Churchill, what kind of woman do you think I am?' And Churchill simply replies, 'Madam, we've already established that. Now we are haggling about the price.'"

A chuckle ran through the room. "Listen. Stop lying to yourself, to your customers. **Accept that functionality is flexible. It's going to change. It can't be frozen up front. Once you accept that, then you can nail down quality, cost, and time. You set high-level functional goals for your project, but with very hard and strict budgets of both time and money.** We've been talking about Sprints in Scrum. You only need to detail the functionality for the next Sprint. That's it. Next Sprint you'll deal with the next bit of functionality. So you can make changes on a dime, but you have to get feedback from your client constantly. By making the functionality dimension flexible, you are forced to look at it over and over. By doing that, you can freeze effort and cost—if you want."

People started to pepper Jerry with questions as soon as he finished. I noticed something interesting as he answered them: he kept changing a question directed to him into a group discussion, asking if anyone in the audience wanted to answer the question. I got what he was trying to do: put the team up front. In the end, his opinion didn't matter; mine as CTO didn't matter; Rick's didn't matter. I saw that he was, albeit subtly, trying to turn the responsibility back on the team. It was a telling habit: he'd really embraced Scrum fully.

I was embarrassed that I was surprised by some of the things that arose from the questions. It turned out some of my own developers were already using some Agile principles. The testers were already doing some sort of daily stand-up meeting to coordinate their work. Most interesting to me was that some of the developers were already organizing mini-Sprint backlogs to distribute work among themselves. Some of them were even timeboxing their work, limiting their efforts to a predetermined number of days. I hadn't even known this kind of thing was happening.

But there was also a lot of skepticism, especially about quality awareness. Some senior developers said they worried Scrum would only be focused on programming, slighting architecture and design.

Frank in particular seemed doubtful. He'd been at the company a while. "Listen," he said, "my job is more than just programming. Hacking together a piece of functionality as fast as you can could really cause problems. What about performance? And maintainability? And, most importantly, quality?"

"Who decides how good your code is?" Jerry asked.

Frank looked a bit taken aback. "I'm sorry?"

"Seriously, who decides? I'll tell you. You do. No one else. You are a professional software engineer. You decide whether you write good code or shitty code. That has nothing to do with what methodology you use. That has to do with how good a programmer you are. Listen, Scrum helps. It helps you to focus on quality by making it visible."

Frank started to say something, but Jerry raised his hand. "No, please, let me finish. First, you have a working product. You can test the quality a lot sooner. And you get to re-do that testing during each Sprint. That says nothing about the quality of the code. But what happens is that each and every member of the team, all of you"—Jerry looked around the room, making eye contact. He continued, "All of you have an obligation to each other to make sure the software is reviewed, re-factored, and compliant to coding standards. And you get to decide what standard to apply. And this happens every Sprint! You can't just bring in quality at the end, when everything is almost finished and you know you have to release the product soon. The pressure is too much. With Scrum, quality is baked in. The check on quality, however you want to arrange it—on maintainability, on quality, refactoring, whatever—is done each and every Sprint. This makes your quality control more transparent and more consistent."

Jerry paused for a second, and Frank seemed thoughtful. Jerry continued, "And I think this is really important," his voice lowered for a moment. "Your own feeling about quality is important. Really important. I can't stress that enough." He gathered himself, stood straighter and continued, "How team members view the quality, subjectively, is a good way to measure how quality changes. And the important part is, that drives conversations. It forces you guys to talk to each other and be honest with one another."

Rick spoke up next. "You never mentioned what a project manager does in Scrum. What's my role in this?"

"There are no project managers in Scrum. There's no need."

"What?" Rick exclaimed, "You mean if we agree to try this, I lose my job?"

"Probably not," replied Jerry calmly. "Companies like yours always need good people who can manage the external side of a project— people who both know the product and can communicate with clients. But inside the project there's no need for a project manager."

"But how do people know what to do?"

"They decide what to do based on the Sprint backlog. Look at it this way: this is an opportunity, not a threat. You'll no longer have to manage the team; they'll do that themselves. Then you can do what is really important, like talking with customers to find out what they really need. And that's a lot more fun than managing developers and solving their problems."

A chuckle rippled through the room.

Jerry laughed too. "It is! With Scrum, on the outside, you manage the expectations of customers and users. But on the inside you manage what the requirements are, what those customers and users are saying they need. This allows every software engineer's talents to be fully utilized—which makes it more fun! Why did you become a project manager in the first place? It wasn't to manage developers, I'll tell you that. It was customer expectations, budget monitoring, deadlines, milestones, coordination, contracts. Focus on that; forget about negotiating scope and workflow. The team and the customer can do a better job of it."

Rick was looking a little glassy-eyed at this point, so I stood up. "Okay, what do you all think? Should we try Scrum? At least on one project?"

Silence. Some folks were nodding their heads. Others were standing with arms crossed. I glanced sidelong at Rick. He was still a little stony-faced.

And then, unexpectedly, George stood up, possibly the youngest person in the room. "I think we should. From a testing point of view, we often don't have enough time to properly test. And even when we find bugs, developers are too busy to fix them. If we work in short cycles we can be much more focused and automate more testing."

He seemed to get both more excited and more confident as he went on. "Think about it. We test more. Developers are more focused on making a stable product. And we can test new features faster. This is a total win."

He sat down, out of breath.

Susan stood then. "I never thought I would say this, but I'm with George one hundred percent. Look, we all know we're in trouble." The room became quiet.

"We are. We all know Mark got his head handed to him by Logistrux last week. And he deserved it. We all deserved it. The product doesn't work! We're late, really late. We have to be honest about this. We can't just pretend everything is hunky dory; it's not! We've got to do something why not Scrum? We don't have much to lose. And heck, I like the idea of being my own boss. No offense, Rick."

"None taken." Rick looked even more uneasy.

I took a quick poll of the room. Most people agreed with Susan. A few senior people were still worried about quality, but sensed the mood of the team. They would go along—at least publicly, I thought. A lot of people were quiet, though, or at least reserved, which was unusual for them. They obviously weren't dead set against it, but Susan's outburst scared them. They knew she was right.

It had been over an hour. "Okay," I said finally. "If everyone's okay with it, we're going to do this on the Logistrux project. Susan's right. We have to do something. And this looks like it may do the trick."

Everyone filed out of the auditorium quietly. But there was something; I couldn't put my finger on it. Maybe they were energized? Maybe this could work.

. . .

I asked Rick and George to stay behind.

"Rick, are you with me on this?" I asked when the doors closed.

"I'm not sure I have a lot of choice, Mark. You seem pretty enthusiastic; the developers and testers," he nodded toward George, "seem behind it." He sighed. "And I know it's bad. Okay. And I know it's been my project. I know you have to do something, so…" He looked up, straight into my eyes. "So let's do this. I'm just not sure what my role is going to be. This 'Scrum Master' thing seems a little too vague to me. Not enough in control, but maybe that's my problem."

"No, you're right, Rick." Jerry tilted his head. **"It's better that a project manager not become the Scrum Master of his project. When a former project manager steps into that role, there's a fair chance that everyone will fall back into their old patterns. The developers will expect him to solve all their problems, and he'll feel obligated to do so."**

"I agree with that, Rick; it's just human nature. But I still want you involved," I said. I felt bad when I saw Rick's shoulders drop with relief. "I'm thinking that you would be perfect for the Product Owner. You understand what needs to be done. Put the team to work, but let them manage themselves. We can have Jerry help train you."

He looked at me gratefully. "Okay, Mark. Let's try it out. Hopefully I can do a better job this time. And Mark," His voice quavered a bit. George and Jerry seemed slightly embarrassed to be in the room. "I'm sorry, Mark. I let you down." He looked at his feet, then back up. "It won't happen again. I'm still not sure about getting the team to take on more responsibility. I feel like I've tried that before and it's never worked. But I'll give it my best."

I put a hand on his shoulder briefly. "That's all I can ask, Rick."

I turned toward George. "I want you to be the Scrum Master."

"Me? But…"

"But what? The team respects you. You've shown leadership. You're easygoing and not a threat to anyone. And you're enthusiastic about this. How about it?"

"Yes." He stammered, excited. "Yes. I'd love to. Thank you."

"I'm going to want you to work with Jerry a lot. I think you can handle this, but I know it's a jump."

"I can do it."

"Good. We start Monday. One of the main things you do as a Scrum Master is remove impediments. Have someone take down these cubicles over the weekend. We don't need to start with things that get in people's way."

Jeff Sutherland, Rini van Solingen, Eelco Rustenburg

the**essentials**

1

Introducing Scrum doesn't require a lot of preparation. Once you pick up the Scrum mind-set you can start immediately. Just do it and make changes based on observations and experiences: Inspect and Adapt.

2

Accept that functionality is flexible and cannot be fixed in detail up front. Such flexibility requires regular feedback.

3

With Scrum you set overall goals for your project or product, with very strict budgets and milestones. The requirements are detailed "just in time" before every sprint.

4

Scrum is not only an adaptation of process, but also of control. Actually, it is a change of culture. The team acquires control and takes on a lot of responsibility.

5

The dynamics and culture of the team are key factors in the implementation of Scrum. Create transparent, explicit expectations and targets for this. Make the team important, and they will act accordingly.

6

Scrum helps you to focus on quality. There is a working product sooner, so you do quality testing earlier, in each and every Sprint.

7

With Scrum, you manage expectations outwards from a project to users and customers, and you manage requirements inwards to the project. Scrum utilizes the full talents of software engineers and therefore they have both more fun and confidence.

8

A 'classic' project manager is not well suited to becoming the Scrum Master. Out of habit, most developers will expect him to solve all their issues.

Chapter 6:
Sprint Preparation

...

Anne and I fought all weekend. I can't even remember what we fought about, but we both knew the real reason. I was making a high-stakes gamble that might or might not save my job. We'd been talking about starting a family, finally. Anne was closer to forty than thirty-five, and the biological clock wasn't in our favor. Neither of us wanted to go the IVF route; we'd seen too many of our friends on that heartbreaking path. But she knew we couldn't start a family if I was out of a job. And given the economy, it might be a while before I could find another one—if I even could find one at the same level.

It wasn't a good weekend. I was already tired when I got to the office Monday morning. I was early again, as much to get out of the house as to get to work. I sat in my office and looked at the calendar. December was that much closer. After the meeting on Friday with Jerry and the team I'd felt buoyed, maybe even excited. Then at about six that night, Dave, the CEO, had called me into his office. I'd been dreading that all week, and it kind of pissed me off that Dave had waited till Friday night to call me in. But that was typical Dave: let you spin for a week, then see if you've come up with a plan. He told me he had spoken with the CEO of Logistrux and knew about the December deadline.

"Can you do it, Mark?" he asked me.

I knew then that I had to put it all on the table. If I didn't, Dave would lose faith in me as CTO. We'd been friends for years, but I could tell he was questioning his own judgment about me.

"I can do it." That was all I said. I didn't talk about Scrum. I didn't give him excuses about Logistrux' change requests. Nothing besides those four words.

Dave just looked at me for a moment, his brown eyes holding my blue ones. I didn't blink. "Okay."

He paused, still looking at me. He picked up some papers from his desk. The gesture of dismissal was unmistakable. "When do you think you'll be able to demo it for me?" He wasn't even looking at me by this point.

"Two weeks." He looked up sharply as I walked out of his office. "See you then."

I snapped back to the present. It had felt good to say that. The doubt didn't even hit me till the drive home.

All right, I thought. Two weeks. We had ten engineers working full time on the Logistrux software. Scrum doctrine prescribed seven plus or minus two. Jerry didn't think that was a problem. The idea was to have small teams, preferably in the same office space.

Of the ten, Susan was their informal leader. Not the manager; more "first among equals." They all took her seriously and followed her lead on architectural issues.

She, George, Rick, Jerry, and I decided on two-week Sprints. We had to get lots of feedback from Logistrux in the next three months, and two-week Sprints would give us that.

I looked up. It was almost eight. I'd been sitting in my office for more than an hour. Jesus. I needed to get a grip. I had to talk to Susan, Rick, and Jerry before the Sprint planning meeting at ten.

· · ·

I walked into the conference room at ten sharp. The team was there. Game face on, I thought, and smiled at Jerry and the team.

"Good morning!" Jerry exclaimed. "Normally, I wouldn't be the one doing the talking. But in this case I want to explain how we're going to organize the Sprints, what is expected from everyone, and what my role will be."

"Rick, Mark, Susan, and I sat down this morning and hashed out the Sprint backlog for the next two weeks. Rick, as the Product Owner, will lay that out in a minute. But I wanted to start by asking you all to really be involved in this first Sprint. We've got a lot to do, so let's skip talking too much about Scrum itself: the whys and the wherefores. For this first Sprint I want you to work exactly as I tell you to. **The best way to learn Scrum and to learn to appreciate it is by applying it 'by the book'. A lot of companies make the mistake of trying to customize Scrum before they understand how it actually works. They nip and tuck, and often erode the philosophy behind Scrum. They think they're using Scrum, but they don't realize what they've lost by taking things out. As a result, they miss out on a lot of what Scrum has to offer.**"

He paused and took a meticulously measured sip of his coffee, just as he'd done at breakfast in London. I found it oddly compelling to watch.

Jerry carefully put the cup down. "Okay, first we're going to have Rick show us the Sprint backlog. Make sure you ask any questions you have. Everything should be crystal clear to the team as to what exactly the Product Owner needs from them this Sprint. We'll do that this morning. After lunch, we'll plan the Sprint. Basically we'll break down the backlog items, or 'stories,' into separate tasks. Each task should take about two to four hours. Once we've done that, and everyone commits to the plan, we can get to work."

He looked around the room. "Yes, it is that simple." Another sip of coffee. "Every day we'll be having a meeting—just a quick one, I promise you. Fifteen minutes tops. But they're really important and I need everyone to be there and to be on time, okay?" He glanced around the room. "George and I will fill the role of Scrum Master this Sprint as he learns the ropes, but we'll get more into that tomorrow."

Another sip of coffee. It was so regular, so precise. "I want you all just to leap in a bit during this first Sprint. I'll explain more as we go along. We all know how much time pressure there is, so we'd better get started. Any questions?" Silence. "Okay, Rick, why don't you start with the Sprint backlog?"

Rick stood up and walked to the front of the room. "All right. I know none of you have done this before, and neither have I, but let's give it a go. Now, we don't really have a product backlog yet that is in line with Scrum principles, and we don't have the time to put one together before this Sprint. But…" He paused. He lowered his voice. "I do think we have enough to run in this first Sprint. We can do this."

Rick then began to present his ideas for the first Sprint on the Logistrux project. **The key was to propose something that could be completed in two weeks, and released as an enhancement to a working product. Each Sprint brought you that much closer toward a real release**.

Of course there was the slight problem that we didn't have a working product at this point. Enhancing disaster didn't seem like the brightest idea, so we'd decided to spend the first Sprint stripping what didn't work out of the product. Rick asked the team to prepare a version that would work with only one database type. Internet functionality? Toss it out. Rick did say that the stripped functionality would be put back in during later Sprints, but that it could be removed for now. The most important thing was to get a releasable and stable product—something we could actually show people.

Rick also wanted them to get the automatic test environment up and running during the Sprint. George had been an advocate, saying the predictability and quality gains would be massive. Rick, as the Product Owner, decided to give that a high priority in this Sprint backlog. He wanted, by the end of the Sprint, to be able to run automated regression tests covering the complete functionality of our product. That way, at the end of each Sprint, it would be clear how much the product had been tested.

The questions began. Mostly they were about exactly what should and should not be removed. They quickly got into far more technical detail than Rick had presented. As I watched Jerry sip his coffee in staccato happiness I realized this was the point. The discussion was what made the presentation valuable. Interesting. Rick had some of the answers, I had a few, and a few we had to decide in the moment. But after forty-five minutes or so, we were all clear on what Rick expected from the team this Sprint.

"Good. Now that we know what's on the Sprint backlog"—Jerry took over again—"the team will now figure out whether that's realistic or not. I'm going to introduce two new ideas here: Velocity and Planning Poker."

Everyone looked at Jerry with some interest. "Velocity is just that: velocity. How fast we're going. To bring you back to high school for a second, if someone asks if you can travel sixty miles in two hours, the first question is…?" He paused for effect, but continued before the groans got too loud. "Yep, what's your velocity? Thirty miles an hour, sure. Four miles an hour, ain't gonna happen."

He brought his cup to his lips for a sip, only to look quizzically at its emptiness. It was the first break in the routine so far. "It's the same thing in Scrum. You've just gotten a certain amount of work from Rick. You have two weeks to complete it. Whether it's feasible to complete the work in the given time depends on the 'velocity' of the team. That is, how much work you, as a team, can get done during a single Sprint. If you know your velocity, you know whether this is a reasonable Sprint backlog.

"In Scrum, we measure velocity by points. Each story is given a number of points by the team. Something really simple might take two points; something more complicated, eight; and something really complicated, a larger number. Now what matters is that people agree on the relative sizing of the stories." Jerry looked so mournfully at his empty coffee cup that I made a note on my phone to have a coffee machine put into the room.

He looked around the room for a second. "You might ask why I don't measure work in hours. That's how everyone else does it, right? This project will take 'x' thousand engineer-hours, and if we divide that up over 'y' weeks we need 'z' number of engineers. Let me just take a minute to explain why that isn't the smartest way of measuring work.

"It's simple, really. George, let's say that you're making, I don't know, paper airplanes."

"Okay."

"I'd bet that for the first few days, you'd be making airplanes at a rate of, let's make a guess…ten an hour."

"I'm pretty sure I could manage that."

"But don't you think you'd get better at it?"

"Huh?"

"I mean, if all you're doing is making paper airplanes, you'd hope you'd get faster at it, right? I mean, over time, you would get quicker, and hopefully, your planes would get better."

"Okay."

"So the first week, you're just learning the ropes; you make four hundred airplanes or so in your forty hours of work."

"All right."

"But the second week you get faster—a lot faster. And you make six hundred airplanes in your forty hours of work."

"I think I see…"

"Wait for it. In the third week, you also make six hundred airplanes in forty hours, but they are demonstrably better than the ones you made in the first or second weeks. Don't you think those should be measured by some other yardstick than hours? If we only count hours, the first and the third weeks are indistinguishable, no?"

"Yeah, I can see that."

"So we want to be able to measure how much faster you get at stories that are about the same difficulty. That's why we use points instead of hours."

"Now, this is the first time you're doing a Sprint, so we're going to have to take a best guess as to how many points you can complete in one two-week period. In future Sprints, we're going to be using points based on the velocity we discover in previous Sprints. And this is very important to remember; using points is the only way we have of measuring how your velocity changes. There are a set number of hours in a week. The question is: how many points you can accomplish in that time?"

Everyone nodded. That made sense, I thought. I'd always measured things in hours. That was how all our accounting was set up, we measured how much everything would cost in terms of hours. I realized that that actually made no sense; it put the wrong incentives in place. I wanted people to get stuff done; that's what made us money. Whether they worked forty or eighty hours on it was pretty immaterial.

I brought my attention back to Jerry. He was explaining "ideal days.""Okay, the real world is not ideal. However, it's easier to estimate when you pretend you're in an ideal world. So, let's begin pretending the world is ideal, then introduce reality."

"There are unicorns?" said George.

"Shut up, George," said Susan.

Jerry chuckled. "So, how much time do you actually spend on the project?"

"Eighty percent" said Susan. "The rest of my time is taken up with other random things."

George spoke up. "For me, it's more like fifty percent. Last minute questions, a quick demo, people wanting me to reproduce a possible error. I have a lot of unpredictable interruptions in my day."

Jerry took a quick poll. The other developers seemed to agree with Susan. They devoted about eighty percent of their time to the project.

"From there," said Jerry, "we just do the math. The Sprint is ten days, minus one for today, the planning day. Nine days left. The last day of the Sprint will be focused on final testing and last-minute issues. So this Sprint really has eight days to work on the project. Ten people on the team, nine at eighty percent, and one at fifty percent." He scribbled some figures on the whiteboard.

He turned back to the room. "The only thing this means is that we are going to work a realistic schedule; we aren't going to work more than we, as a team, think we can realistically handle. We will know what our baseline velocity is in two weeks."

He pulled a deck of cards from his pocket. "And to figure out what we think is reasonable, everyone's favorite game: Planning Poker!" He said it with a flourish.

Silence.

Jerry quickly moved on. "You all know the Fibonacci sequence, right? This is loosely based on that. The cards go 0, ½, 1, 2, 3, 5, 8, 13, 20, 40, 100. Mainly, I think, because the maker can't copyright the Fibonacci sequence." He laid out the cards on the table; there were ten or so of each number. "Now, everyone take a full set, and what we're going to do is give our best estimate for how many points each story is going to take."

He passed out the cards. "Planning Poker is based on group consensus. Each one of us will independently estimate each item on the Sprint backlog. We'll talk about the different estimates, and then we'll play another round. We'll do as many rounds as it takes until everyone agrees. Sound good?"

Everyone seemed to at least like the idea of playing cards during the work day, I thought.

"Let's take a look at the easiest story on Rick's backlog. We are going to make that our reference story, and we'll estimate every other story by comparing it to that story. Three points is a good number to give the reference story."

The team looked through the backlog, found an easy story and gave it a 3.

"The top item on Rick's backlog is 'XML export of all data in the database.' Don't consult, don't show your cards to anyone else; this is poker, after all. Just think how many points you think that will take compared to the reference story. Put that card on the table face down."

Just about everyone nodded, sorted through their cards and picked one out. Brian, the joker in the group, put on his shades and slumped down, dramatically slapping his card on the table. Everyone chuckled and did their own poker play imitations.

Jerry looked at everyone with exaggerated intensity. "Okay, everyone, show your cards!"

They flipped them over. A few question marks, indicating they had no idea; lots of 40's; two people put 100; and Susan, surprisingly, turned over an 8.

"Great," said Jerry. "You disagree. Perfect." I thought he was actually going to rub his hands together. "This is good. No, seriously. Let's see what the arguments between the extremes are. George, why'd you estimate 100?"

"Well, I was really thinking about sixty hours because I don't understand points, but there's not a 60 card, so I rounded up. I think we need that much time because we'll need at least a solid week of sound testing on a lot of different databases. Building doesn't seem that complicated, but the testing would be extensive."

"Susan, why an eight?"

"Well," Susan said, "I actually wrote an XML export a few months ago. I got a question about connecting our system with a piece of software I didn't really know, but it did have an XML import function. I had to do this on the side, outside of my normal job, so I didn't have a lot of time, but I was able to find some open source stuff that runs on the most common databases. I got it working fairly fast, sent it off to the customer, and it worked! I still need to do some work to tidy it up, integrate it properly, and document it. I think it's smart to make some automated tests for this, like George suggested, and that would take a bit more time…let me see…"

"Stop there!" Jerry shouted. "Now that we've talked about the rationales, it's time for another round. It's important in Planning Poker that one person's estimate doesn't influence another's. Oh, and George, you don't have to round up; if it's 40 or 100, choose the number that fits best. We're not playing Price is Right rules. Okay, one more time."

Everyone thought for a moment, then put their cards on the table again. Everyone had twenty except for Susan, who put down a thirteen, but then exclaimed, "No, that's good, twenty works!" and quickly changed her card to reflect that.

The coffee that I had texted my secretary to get from Chinatown Coffee came in. Chinatown's expensive, but as much as I hate to admit it, those coffee hipsters make a damn good cup of coffee. I'd also told her to get a cart ready for later.

"Chinatown, boss?" asked Rick.

"Don't get used to it," I growled.

Everyone sorted out their coffee, even the heathens who put in milk. I carefully watched Jerry pour himself a cup. *Hmm. It's just the drinking that's done with robotic precision.*

"So that's Planning Poker," said Jerry. "We keep doing rounds of this until there is a consensus on the estimates. Any differing estimates are talked about. How, why, what you don't understand. You want to make sure that nothing is missed or forgotten. **Differences in estimates are good! The true value of Planning Poker is in the discussions, not the numbers. By talking about it extensively, we ensure that we, as a group, don't overlook anything—that we really understand what needs to be done. The real value of this estimating is not a correct prediction, but making sure that the work in a Sprint runs predictably.**"

He took a sip of coffee. Exactly the same. It was uncanny. "Predictability of Sprint output is essential. And you'll get better at it. We'll compare the estimates we make now to what we actually do at the end, and then use that data to improve our next estimates. That way, you'll know your velocity, and then you'll start to increase it and you'll get better, as a team, at estimating what you can do."

With that, the team got down to business, quickly estimating each story on the Sprint backlog in points. As expected, there was more than they thought could be done in one Sprint. But Rick prioritized the list, so the team took the top things that they estimated they could do in the Sprint, dropping the two bottom items off. Those items were the lowest priority, so that seemed fine. When they were done, the stories added up to forty-two points. Jerry said, "Forty-two is your estimated velocity. For the first Sprint, there may be some startup costs. Practical experience shows this might be as much as forty percent in the first Sprint. Also, we know that it is important for the team to feel successful, as successful teams improve more quickly. Take fewer points. If you finish early you can always pull more stories from the product backlog into the Sprint." The team decided on thirty points.

The entire estimation exercise took less than two hours. I felt pretty good at the end. Everyone understood what to do, how to do it, and how big a job it might be. I wanted them to take more work into the Sprint because we were behind, but Jerry had warned me that rapid improvement of team performance depended on not overloading the team. A realistic schedule for the next two weeks was worked out. Rick used to need a week to do that. Not bad for a morning's work.

But then I thought, *This may only work this once.* Everyone already knew what the product had to do. We weren't actually going to build anything this Sprint; we were going to tear out the stuff that didn't work. Next time we would be adding new features. I rested my palms flat on the table and looked at my hands. I hoped those next meetings went as smoothly. At the end of this Sprint we'd have about nine weeks left.

I looked up as Rick took the floor again. "Do you all think you can accomplish this in the next two weeks?"

Everyone nodded.

"Okay, then, go to it. See you in two weeks! Good luck!"

"Not so fast, Rick!" Jerry spoke out. "We're not done for today yet. Everything is clear as to what has to be done, but that's on the story level. Now we need to break that down into individual tasks: things that will take a couple of hours. The team needs that kind of granularity so that everyone knows, in detail, what they should do over the next two weeks. It also helps us double-check our estimates. For beginning teams, it's useful to break the stories down into specific technical tasks and estimate the tasks in hours. That will further clarify the work and flush out more details. We can then add up the hours and see if we have enough hours available from the team. We're all in this together, and that includes you, Mr. Product Owner!"

Rick sat back down, grinning. It was good to see him smiling.

"And," Jerry said, "your work as Product Owner isn't done yet. This is something you need to get. You don't just vanish for two weeks and come back and see what the team has done. The Product Owner has to be continually involved and always be available to answer questions. Things might come up over the next two weeks that need to be answered, and you need to answer them to make sure the result is viable and valuable. Everything that's unclear, and any further choices that need to be made, have to go through the Product Owner."

"That makes sense," said Rick.

"Good. Now during this next part of breaking down the stories into tasks, you aren't to take a leading role. This is the team's work. But you need to be here if questions come up as they do their work. You're not in a leading role, but a serving one." He fixed Rick with a look that seemed to communicate a little more deeply than his jovial personality might have led you to expect. "It's noon. Let's break for lunch and then come back and continue."

. . .

Everyone was back in the conference room before one p.m. While we were out, Jerry had covered the walls with large sheets of paper. Each sheet had one backlog item at the top. Next to each item was the estimate of how long it would take.

"Welcome back!" Jerry said as the last of us filed in. "What we're going to do now is called the second part of the Sprint Planning Meeting. We're going to break down all of these stories"—he waved to the piece of paper—"into separate chunks of work. The reason we're going to do this is that we're doing this project as a team, together. To do that, we all have to agree on exactly what needs to be done. And we need to know that everyone can always work on something that is a concrete step toward the Sprint goal."

He walked toward one piece of paper. "We're going to cut the work into digestible chunks. **Ideally, each task to be done would take two to four hours. So, ideally, you can finish two to four tasks completely each day. That way you're always working toward concrete intermediate goals and targets.** Here's why you want to do this: **at the end of each day you get to go home knowing you accomplished something.** How many times have you gone home and sort of felt, *well, I think I moved the project forward today, I worked hard anyway,* but you can't point at one thing and say, *I did that. It's done.*"

That feeling was an uncomfortable partner at times. I could remember days when self-doubt would sit on my shoulder and whisper, "Did you really do anything today? Or were you just pretending? You faker. They're going to find out you're a phony, you know." I could see that having concrete deliverables every day would make my progress clear to myself and also to the group. And, it occurred to me, that progress could be measured.

"Each of these pieces of paper has one story on it. I want you all to split up into groups of two or three and start breaking them down. This is your Sprint, so Rick, Mark, and I won't interfere. If you find that you can't break a story down into chunks smaller than, say, eight hours, then the story is too big; we need to split it into two or more. As you're doing this, start thinking about a calendar and some detailed planning for the next two weeks."

Groups formed awkwardly, with much glancing and nodding. George took the lead, though. He's impressive for a young guy. He's worked with all of the developers and seems to have a knack for knowing which ones are better at certain problems. He didn't tell them, he questioned them—and over the course of a few minutes, without being told to, pretty much all the right people were standing in front of the right pieces of paper.

Everyone started a bit awkwardly, but as people began to engage, it became dynamic. These were professional engineers, after all, and they'd just been asked to give their professional opinion, something most software developers are more than willing to share even at inappropriate times. A few times, an engineer left the room to look something up. Sometimes an engineer from one group would be pulled into another group's discussion. It was a bit tricky specifying the work without knowing all the technical details, but it worked. A few hours later the sheets of paper were full of lists of tasks. Each time a group finished, Jerry split them up and sent them to work with other teams on other stories.

"Okay, everyone go out and get some more of that coffee. And bring some back for me too; that was damned good coffee," said Jerry. "George and I have a bit of work to do."

Jerry and George took the sheets down and put all the stories and tasks into a spreadsheet while everyone else ran to Chinatown Coffee.

• • •

By the time they got back, Jerry and George had the spreadsheet projected onto a screen.

"We're almost done," said Jerry. "Now we just need to estimate the amount of effort each task will take. We can use Planning Poker if we have to, but let's try and estimate directly. Okay?"

Almost every task broke down into a few hours of work. There were two anomalies, estimated at three days. The team explained that they'd picked three days because they needed to do a technical feasibility study that could last from one to three days, so they picked the worst case scenario. Jerry nodded. "It's not ideal. But for this first Sprint, let's accept it and move on."

George entered in the new estimates and added up the cells to see if the task estimates fit the number of hours available from the team. Some stories looked bigger after the tasks were detailed out, but others looked smaller. Surprisingly to me, the total fit in closely with the velocity we thought we could do.

"This is great; I'm really proud of you." Jerry beamed from his chair. "It took one day, and you have a complete and detailed schedule of tasks, and you all agree on it, as a team. Enough from me for today; you guys can get to work."

George sat up, shocked. "But Jerry, we haven't agreed on who will do what. And what about the dependencies? A lot of these tasks lean on each other. I don't think we're finished at all!"

"George, you're kind of right, but you're kind of wrong too," Jerry replied. "We are ready with the plan, but I haven't explained how we're going to use this plan. I also need you all, as a team, to commit to this plan. But first, let me explain how we're going to organize the rest of the Sprint."

He fiddled with his laptop for a second and a new image appeared on the screen. "This is what we call a Scrum Board."

"It's fairly straightforward. Three columns: To Do, Busy, Done. We put each story into the To Do section, in prioritized order on sticky notes or index cards. The ones at the top are the most important, the next most important, and so on. Then the tasks are put with the right stories. When you start work on a task, you take the task and put it into the Busy column. Everyone gets to decide which task to work on individually. But!" Jerry slapped the table to wake us up out of our late afternoon drowsiness, which had set in despite how much coffee we had drunk. "You're part of a team! No cherry picking. Take those tasks that you're most suited to, are most important at the time, and that you can finish within the scheduled time. Trust me, the Scrum Board is now your new water cooler; it's where you'll be having all your discussions about progress and aligning work. It's fun.

"Another thing that is really important is testing. We need the software to work at the end of the Sprint, so we can get feedback and prove that it's possible to deliver the software on a tight schedule. If we wait too long to test each story, there will be too much testing piled up at the end of the Sprint, and the Sprint will not be successful. So the biggest challenge for the team is to complete the tasks for the top story as soon as possible, including testing. This means that people will need to work together to make this happen.

"Simply put," he said, **"during this Sprint you will, as a team, move the whole pile of separate tasks, together, shoulder-to-shoulder, to the Done column. Sounds a little bit like a scrum in rugby, no?"**

Everyone looked around at each other. I could feel them starting to realize that they were part of a team. Today had begun that process. I could see it. They weren't totally comfortable with it.

Jerry stood up. "Here's what I want you to do. I want you to commit to this Sprint, as a team. I want you to be committed together. You know how much is riding on this. Mark has been pretty open about the situation. But you can't do it alone. You can't do it using the old way. You need to commit to this Sprint, together, totally. I want you to be completely inflexible about the work in this Sprint. This is what you will get done. Nothing more. Nothing less. Nothing different. What we've all agreed to today.

"But that certainty needs something from you, collectively: your commitment—commitment to this work, to this backlog, and to each other. You have to make a promise. I promised you all you could stop lying. Here's your chance. Commit to this. It's a stable product, with a limited feature set that has to work right."

He looked at each one of them—and me. "I can't do it for you."

He stopped for a moment, then continued. "I can't do it for you. You have to make that decision, that promise to yourself, to your team, to Rick, to Mark. I want each of you to say it, and each of you to hear it: a commitment to doing this Sprint. Susan?"

"Yes, I'm committed."

"George?"

"Yes, I promise." And so it went around the room: one by one, they all committed to it. It's an odd thing when a group of people pledge to each other they will do something together. There's an almost palpable sense of that commitment, a vibration in the room; a new thing has been evoked into being.

Everyone else felt it too. The pressure was there, but there was a sense of elation, of relief too. There was a way out.

"Okay," said Jerry seriously. "Okay, let's do it."

"Wait!" I interrupted. "This requires a celebration. We've started something new today, and it deserves a toast."

I got the cart with the champagne from outside the door. The corks popped, the bubbly poured, and a toast was raised. I felt good for the first time in a long while.

the**essentials**

1

You can learn to apply and appreciate Scrum best by doing it "by the book."

2

A big mistake many organizations make is to start customizing Scrum before they've even started. Key concepts may be missed, which jeopardizes the real value that Scrum has to offer.

3

Velocity is the amount of work a team can tackle during a Sprint. Only by knowing their velocity can a team accurately estimate how much work they can get done in a single Sprint.

4

Planning Poker is the estimation technique used in Scrum. Each team member privately estimates how much work any particular item will require. The team then shares those estimates with each other and discusses any differences until they reach consensus.

5

Differences in estimates at Planning Poker are opportunities. Discussing the differences helps the team better understand the tasks. The rationales behind differing estimates are important to discuss. The learning from these discussions is in fact far more significant than the estimates themselves.

6

The essence of planning is to become predictable. Comparing estimates against reality facilitates learning.

7

Alignment of work is done via the "Scrum Board." This board has 3 sections: "To Do," "Busy," and "Done." During a Sprint, all items are processed from "To Do," via "Busy," to "Done." At the end of the sprint all Items should be in "Done."

8

On the Scrum Board, the team has a constant and clear view of the Sprint status and progress. Work-items are laid out in a prioritized and dependent order. The item on top is most important.

Chapter 7:
During the Sprint

...

I didn't get home till late Monday. After the meeting, I spent hours in the office catching up on our other projects. On the drive home it was dark. I felt a slight malaise grip me. The meeting had gone well. Or it had seemed to, anyway. But what did I know? Had I just wasted the past week on some pie-in-the-sky effort that wouldn't work?

As I pulled up, the lights were out in the house. I was gripped by an odd moment of panic that Anne had left. That there would be a note on the table, or something else equally clichéd, that would wrench my life apart. I unlocked the door with a hand that trembled, telling myself I was being ridiculous.

I walked into the dark house. It was quiet, only the sounds of the house itself were present. I, stood in the kitchen, and just listened. The place creaked and moved and hummed, almost as if it lived. I couldn't hear anything except the house. I set my keys down, then my bag, and walked upstairs into the bedroom. There she was, sound asleep. Her dark hair spilled over the pillow like a black river frozen in motion. I quietly got undressed, didn't even brush my teeth. Got under the covers and lay there, listening to her and the house breathe around me.

...

I woke up before Anne and slipped out while she was still sleeping. She looked so beautiful asleep that I couldn't bring myself to wake her up and fight with her. I'm fairly sure she felt something similar and was feigning sleep when I went downstairs.

I drove into town and picked up Jerry at the hotel. He began instantly to do a postmortem of the day before. He was excited, but expressed some doubts about Rick. He thought Rick was underestimating the changes that were coming his way, and what he was going to have to do to be a successful Product Owner.

I was noncommittal. I thought Rick at least knew what was at stake, even if he didn't know quite how to work through his new role. I told Jerry that none of us really understood the roles yet, and to give Rick a chance to prove himself. He deserved it.

George was there early as well. He and Jerry quickly set up the Scrum board and put it on a pillar in the middle of the developer's space. The large whiteboard was divided into three sections: "To Do," "Busy," and "Done." The "To Do" box quickly filled up with Post-Its. Each one denoted an individual task and the estimated effort it would take. I noticed there was space on each note to write down the actual effort needed as well. *That's smart*, I thought. *Afterward the team can check their estimates with reality.*

Everyone was there at nine sharp, just as Jerry had asked—except for Rick. *Wonderful*, I thought.

Jerry quickly went through how to use the Scrum board—quickly, because there wasn't much to it. "Take an item, move it to 'Busy' while you're working on it, then to 'Done' when it's, well, done. Mark your name on the item so everyone knows who is working on what."

He wrapped up: **"Since all the tasks are listed in order of priority, you work from top to bottom, from left to right during the Sprint. Imagine the team as a snowplow that pushes the tasks from the top left of the board to the bottom right. Once all the tasks are in the 'Done' column, then the Sprint is over. Simple enough,** eh?"

No one said anything. Rick walked in at that point and tried to quietly take a seat.

"Good Let's move on. We're burning daylight. I'll lead the first stand-up meeting, or 'Daily Scrum.' We're going to be having our Scrum every day at nine sharp. It is crucial"—a sharp glance at Rick—"that everyone be here, and be on time."

Rick at least had the grace to look a bit embarrassed. I glared at him until he looked at me. At least he looked a little sheepish. I thought maybe Jerry had had a point earlier. We'd see.

"Listen," said Jerry. "Arriving late at the stand-up puts the objective of the meeting at risk. The objective? Make sure the team has a good a day as possible. When the whistle blows, everyone's on the field, no? If they aren't, they not only might lose the game; they would deserve to lose. They weren't taking it seriously. Being part of a team means you've made commitments to each other. Live up to them. Let's start with nine as the meeting time, okay? If for some real reason people can't get here at that time, it's better to actually move the meeting time so everyone isn't just waiting around for someone else. **The purpose of the stand-up is to coordinate the team, and we can't do that if people aren't here.**"

"These meetings are short, but they require your concentration and your energy. No more than fifteen minutes, but I need you to be active! No leaning against the wall, no sitting down. The idea is that you are here, in this meeting, mind and body. If you have trouble concentrating for fifteen minutes, you either have a dosage problem or a commitment problem. Fix it."

He looked at each of them for a moment. "I'm going to act as Scrum Master today, but George will take over the role tomorrow. You've all seen the tasks, so I'm going to ask you the three questions you're going to be asked every day: What did you do yesterday to help the team reach the Sprint goal? How are you going to help the team today? And what got in your way?"

"I'm going to ask each one of you these questions, okay?"

"I had a few brews yesterday." Jim cracks.

"Come on, we only have fifteen minutes; let's use the time effectively. Focus, please. What did you do to help the team meet the Sprint goal?"

It turned out Jim had actually stayed late yesterday to get started on something. As he talked, Jerry moved the task from the To Do column into Busy. Jim had also run into a bug.

"Good, you reported it. But try only to mention things that will block the Sprint, the ones that jeopardize meeting our goal. Will this bug impact the Sprint goal? Do you need help from the team?"

"No," Jim said, "I think I can handle it."

Jerry nodded. "Great. Try to keep focused on the Sprint during these meetings. Share with the team what you're doing, what you've achieved, and when you're dependent on them for something. Mention the problems that put the Sprint at risk. We're working in a field that can't be completely planned out. The unexpected will always crop up. What we can do, though, is make sure we bring these things to light so we can address and resolve them as soon as possible."

"Problems you can't resolve that threaten the Sprint are called 'impediments.' At the standup meeting, they'll be assigned to someone; usually the Scrum Master takes the lead. It's important that the impediments be resolved that day! Either by reassigning work, rescheduling, talking to the Product Owner about priorities, whatever. It doesn't matter what the solution is, just make sure it's solved by the next day. That way the Sprint keeps on track, so you all are always working to a plan that actually is feasible."

About fifteen minutes had gone by. "That's pretty much it. Just one word of warning: keep focused on one task; don't move a bunch of them into Busy at the same time. You will work more efficiently. Okay, get to it!"

Jerry and George and I sat down for a few minutes after the meeting. Jerry pointed out to George that the Scrum board would become the center of the room; it was where people would congregate to talk about problems and tasks. He also said that in the standup, the discussion was the real goal, and more important than the outcome. George nodded. I asked him if he felt comfortable stepping into the Scrum Master role the next day.

"I think so, but I'd like Jerry around to give me some pointers."

"Of course," said Jerry.

"And…" George looked at me with some trepidation.

"What?" I said as gently as I could muster.

"Well, I'm not sure if Rick is really letting go of the whole 'I'm the boss' thing. I'm worried about disagreeing with him in front of the team."

I looked at him for a moment. "Let me worry about Rick."

"Okay."

. . .

I returned to my office after the meeting. I tried to call Anne at work and then on her cell. No answer. Shit.

. . .

I walked back into the development area after lunch. Jerry and George were working on what Jerry called a "Burn-down Chart."

"The idea," said Jerry to George, "is to be able to look at one graph and see how the Sprint is going. You want the team to see, in a single glance, where they are, how they're doing, and if the Sprint is going off track."

He quickly sketched a rough graph on a piece of paper. "A burn-down chart shows how fast the team is 'burning' the time they have in the Sprint versus how much stuff was supposed to get done in that time. So, on the bottom axis, I'll draw the number of days in the Sprint. Here we have eight real working days. The first day of the two weeks was taken up with planning, and the last day will be taken up with evaluation. So, eight days."

He drew the y-axis up and down. "And here is the amount of work we have. Remember, we agreed on 61 days of work for the whole team: 488 hours' worth of work was planned." He drew a straight line from the upper left to the bottom right. "Okay, that's what would ideally happen. Each real day would go exactly as we predicted it and it would evenly burn down to the last day of the Sprint."

He looked at George and me. "You both know that's not going to happen, right?"

I grinned. George looked a bit startled. "Some days you'll get more done, some less. What you need to do as Scrum Master, George, is put a dot on the chart that shows the estimated effort that is still needed. Everything in the To-Do and Busy lines. Don't count anything as half-done; it's not done until it's done."

"Okay," said George. "But the line will deviate."

"Yup. It can go like this." Jerry drew a curve below the line. "That means things are going ahead of schedule. Or it can go like this." He drew a curve above the line. "And that means things aren't going so well."

"But what do we do if it's not working?"

"That's situational, and hopefully we won't get there. But what the burn-down chart does is give us the ability to see if that's happening, and tell us we need to adjust."

George looked at the two graphs. "Got it. Rick always used to have these traffic light indicators to show how things were going, which I never quite understood. This is clear. Thanks."

"No problem," grinned Jerry.

. . .

Anne was cooking dinner when I got home. It was weird—like nothing had happened. She was cheerful and happy. She asked about my day, told me about hers, mentioned Thanksgiving plans. The whole night was like that. We watched a movie and went to bed together. It felt like I was an actor in my own body. That I wasn't really there, that the past few days I had lived through were different than the ones she had.

I didn't say anything. It was like the whole night was made out of crystal and I didn't want to crack it.

. . .

I got in early again the next morning. I was curious what people were thinking about Scrum. Ten minutes before the standup, I was at the Scrum board with Jerry and George. The rest of the team trickled in, Rick last of all. I glanced at the clock: nine sharp. At least he was improving.

George took the lead. "Good morning. Thanks for being on time. I'll be leading these from now on, so let's just jump right in. Susan? What did you get done since yesterday's standup?"

Susan quickly answered all three questions: What have you done to help the team meet the Sprint goal since yesterday? What are you going to do today? What is standing in your way? Every team member responded to the questions, one by one. Some people had gotten more done than others. But what I thought was most valuable was that they were focused on what they'd achieved, and could achieve, in a single day. As each day went by, I could see that they would become more and more aware of what they spent their time on, and what they could actually accomplish in a day.

As the team continued to report, I thought about what they were doing. It does make a difference when someone reports that something is complete, done. Not half done, not almost all the way done. Done. In twenty-four hours these people had accomplished real work toward a concrete goal. I could actually hear the excitement from some of them. It was fun to get things done.

But not everyone was happy. When Vince's turn came around, he obviously wasn't engaged. George asked him the questions. He was leaning against a cube and looking at the ground. Vince was one of the more senior people on the team, and someone I had pegged for trouble.

"Come on, Vince!" snapped George. "Be an active part of this meeting. Stand up and talk to the team!"

"Listen, newbie, I've been doing this since you were a teenager. I'm certainly not going to be questioned by a tester! I'm working on something a little more complicated than you can handle, and I think I'm going to go get some real work done." With that, Vince started to walk away.

Jerry put a hand on my arm before I exploded. "Vince, hold on a sec. Come back, please?"

Vince turned around and looked at Jerry. I'm sure he could see me fuming as well. Jerry spoke quickly to try and defuse the situation.

"Vince, we're not finished. You're part of this team and belong in this meeting. I hear your frustration. I hear that you feel it's not useful to you today. But it is really useful for your colleagues to hear what you're working on. It's not going to take hours, just a few minutes, okay?"

Vince stepped back into the circle. Reluctantly, but he did it. He very carefully didn't look at me.

"Sorry about that, but I had to intervene," said Jerry. "You all have to realize that George is the Scrum Master, but he isn't the boss or the project manager. He's a facilitator. He may ask the questions, but you don't report to him. You report to each other."

Jerry spoke very calmly, and very clearly, trying to turn the energy in the room. "George's job is to make sure the Scrum process runs smoothly and that you all can do what you need to do. Use him. Use this opportunity. Tell the team your problems so we all can help you fix them. That will certainly save you more than fifteen minutes each day."

Jerry stepped into the circle and made eye contact with the group. "You are your own bosses now. There is no project manager. No one is going to tell you what to do every day. You're all adults. You all," he swept his arm to take them all in, "are the project leaders. You all need to be familiar with each other's work. It's the only way this will work. Trust me on this. I've seen this before. You'll start to value these meetings as you get used to them. It takes a little faith, but just try it for a bit. Remember, yesterday you all committed to this. You gave your word. Show me you can keep it, at least for a few weeks, okay?"

He turned to Vince. "Can you do that, Vince?"

Vince had cooled down a bit. "Okay, but if it's not working in a couple of weeks, I'm going to bring it up with Mark."

'Mark has nothing to say about these meetings."

I raised an eyebrow at Jerry, but he kept going, obviously assuming I'd get the message and not butt in.

"Listen! You own your work practices now. At the end of each Sprint we'll evaluate and decide together what needs to be changed. If you, as a team, decide to stop doing stand-ups, you can do that. But think very carefully before you do. Every element of Scrum is there for a reason. There aren't that many elements, and they've been reduced to their essence; everything is necessary. So don't start getting rid of something just because you don't like it at first blush. I've seen teams do that. They're doing Scrum, but they decide they're not doing this or that. You can decide to do that. But believe me, you will not produce as much software as fast. I can show you the research if you want, or you can trust me. If you want to really accelerate, you need to embrace the whole program. Try it. Let's revisit it in a couple weeks at the end of the Sprint. The core principle, though, is that you, as a team, own your own processes."

Everyone looked thoughtful, even Vince. "Here's why Mark doesn't have anything to say about these meetings. He's the CTO. He needs to only be concerned with strategic issues. He can only ask that you use Scrum. He can't decide it for you. You own your work processes. Rick also stands outside. As the Product Owner, he's concerned with what comes out of the process, not what happens within it. Now this can be hard. You're being asked to take responsibility for yourselves—to show that you can control your own processes. You can show that you deserve that responsibility, or not. How you show it is by finishing what's on the Sprint backlog, the backlog that you all committed to yesterday. Mark and Rick don't care how you deliver the product; they only care that it is delivered. Does that make sense to everyone?"

They all nodded.

George spoke up. "Sorry for being confrontational, Vince. I know you're senior and I respect that. I didn't mean to upset you. I'm trying to figure this out too."

"It's okay, kid."

My respect for George rose a few notches when he didn't rise to that. "Could you just tell us, briefly, what you did yesterday, what you're going to do today, and what got in your way?"

Vince gave a little more this time. The task he was working on had already taken four hours more than estimated. He was struggling with some difficult regular expressions, and fell into the old trap of trying to solve delays by working harder. Probably why he was irritable in the first place.

Brian, another developer who was usually pretty quiet, spoke up. His Master's thesis was on regular expressions, and it quickly became apparent he could help Vince. It came to light that they'd never talked about this before, and Vince had had no idea that regular expressions was Brian's area of expertise.

I watched silently as the team came together with a plan of action. Jerry winked at me. I nodded. This was actually working!

I looked at the team, engaged with one another, and realized that developers rarely ever simply talked to each other about problems they were having. They used to just tell Rick about their issues, and almost never asked each other for help. Rick would usually reassign the task to someone else or give the person more time. *Take out the middleman*, I thought, *take out the middleman*.

The stand-up was over. George took a few minutes to explain the burn-down chart, and then Jerry asked everyone to get there a bit early the next day as he had something to go over before the stand-up.

...

I looked at the clock. 6:30. It was time to go home. It was hard to bring myself to shut down my computer and head out.

On the way home I thought about Anne. It felt like we were stuck, our roles in glass. We couldn't move and change around one another. I was the successful one, the breadwinner, the guy who couldn't fail. And yet I had failed, more than once. Each time we'd had to move. But we still pretended that I hadn't failed: it was just bad timing, the market wasn't there, my partner had turned out to be untrustworthy. Sure, there had been successes too; I wouldn't be CTO of a major firm if there hadn't been. But the last few years had been rough, and yet we were still pretending I was the golden boy.

She was scared. Heck, I was scared. If this project failed, our mutually agreed-upon lie would be shown for what it was. But we'd been doing the same thing the same way for so long, it was hard to even think about another way of being—of another role to play in my marriage. I didn't even like the one I was playing anymore, but I didn't know how to stop any more than she did.

She wasn't home when I got there. I got a text from her on the way home saying she'd be at the office late. I ordered a pizza, ate, and then went to bed.

. . .

I snuck out early the next morning. I pretended to be quiet and she pretended to be asleep. I knew it was the wrong thing to do. I wanted to say something, but I just couldn't.

. . .

Everyone was there by 8:30. It was a relief when they came in. I'd been there since seven.

Jerry hung a large sheet of paper on the wall. As soon as everyone gathered he began. "What does 'done' mean?"

Everyone looked around. "Finished?" guessed George.

"Okay. What do we mean by finished? You all are working hard on the tasks on the backlog. How do you know when you're finished? In Scrum we have a way of answering that question. We list criteria that the product must meet in order to say it's finished. We call that the 'Definition of Done.' We use this Definition of Done, DoD for short, so we don't miss anything. Functionality? Check. Tested? Check. Quality? Check. That kind of thing. Normally you'd use the DoD during Sprint planning to make sure you've defined all the tasks completely, but we didn't have one, and I didn't want to overload you at first. But as we are starting to complete tasks"—he pointed to the Scrum board—"we need to have a Definition of Done."

Jerry asked every member of the team how they decided when something was 'done,' writing all their answers down on the piece of paper. He also asked Rick, because as the Product Owner, said Jerry, he got to define what he saw as done. Jerry went around again, making sure everyone had listed all the requirements for "done" that they could think of. I noticed he was grouping the ideas into separate clusters.

I realized he'd probably done this enough times that he already knew what people were going to say. When the list was finished he turned to Rick, as Product Owner, to help prioritize it. At the end, he said, there should be a prioritized list that everyone could agree meant "done."

"That's a lot of stuff," Jerry finally said. "Tell you what, for this Sprint let's just take the top five." He wrote them down on a piece of paper and taped it to the Scrum board.

"One thing," Jerry turned back to the group, "This 'Definition of Done' only applies to this Sprint. After it's over, we'll re-evaluate. The last day of the Sprint we'll do a 'Sprint Retrospective' and go over everything that happened, including the 'Definition of Done,' to see if it works. And this definition is limited, which is okay for this Sprint; just be aware of it. But at least we've defined 'done.'"

I was startled to realize that this "Definition of Done" actually answered all the worries I had had about the lack of documentation as far back as my trip to London. If the DoD required adequate documentation, that would have to be delivered within each Sprint. This would actually be better; we used to document everything after the fact, when we were under the gun to deliver, and no one thought it was important. I began to understand why Jerry called Scrum a "kind of magic" back in London. Things were just falling into place. I could see the detail and discipline it would force us to undertake. I'd never seen anything like it before.

George started the stand-up right after the "Definition of Done." Vince's issue, with Brian's help, had been solved. They actually had made some progress on other tasks that involved regular expressions.

Then Susan spoke up. "Hey, our 'Definition of Done' includes making an installer for the product. We didn't even talk about that in the Sprint planning meeting; that's going to take a lot of time."

"Let me take that on as an impediment and see what I can do," said George. "Fair enough?"

The team gave its assent and the meeting broke up.

George and Rick sat down right afterward and went over the installer issue. They decided that for this Sprint, the installer wasn't critical, as we weren't going to be releasing the product at the end. But, Rick cautioned, that wouldn't be the case with the next Sprint, and it would be on the backlog for sure. George nodded. Impediment resolved.

"If the Product Owner agrees"—Jerry sipped his coffee—"then we put it in as part of the DoD improvement for the next Sprint."

Rick nodded.

I felt that things were starting to move. This might actually work. I pulled up the calendar on my phone and began counting Sprints to December.

Then I thought of Anne and remembered our anniversary was Sunday. How in hell had I forgotten that?

Jeff Sutherland, Rini van Solingen, Eelco Rustenburg

the**essentials**

1

On the Scrum board, all work-items are listed in prioritized order. The team processes the Scrum board from top left to bottom right. Just as with a snowplow, the board is cleared.

2

The Scrum board is an important meeting place. As with Planning Poker, the discussion itself is the most important thing. The discussion contributes to understanding and coordination within the team. Using the board triggers these discussions and makes them happen.

3

On a burn-down chart you visually show how quickly the team "burns" their scheduled hours in relation to the amount of work that needs to be done. The team can see their progress in a single glance.

4

To determine if something is really "finished" and whether it meets the predetermined quality criteria, Scrum uses a tool: the Definition of Done (DoD). The DoD is a list of criteria that is used as a checklist to ensure that nothing is forgotten and that the work is truly finished.

5

The DoD is also used in the Sprint Planning Meeting to assess whether the team has completely defined all necessary work-items.

6

Scrum helps you to focus on quality. There is a working product sooner, so you do quality testing earlier, in each and every Sprint.

7

The Product Owner determines only what comes out of the process, not how that process is *formed*. The Product Owner does not determine the working process of the development team; this they decide upon themselves. They earn the right to this ownership by delivering, at the end of each Sprint, what they have committed to on the Sprint backlog.

8

The fact that a Scrum team focuses on what is being, and what can be, achieved each day, increases their time awareness. Putting emphasis on what has been achieved has the advantage that there is a clear focus on getting results.

Chapter 8:
Preparing the Next Sprint

...

Jerry sat down with Rick and me that afternoon. We were just a few days into the Sprint, but the beginning of the next Sprint was only a little more than a week away. Two weeks goes fast. Rick needed to put together a carefully groomed backlog before the next Sprint started. Jerry wanted me there to get a better grasp on how to build a good backlog, and to make any strategic decisions that might arise

"Okay, Rick, everyone else is working; now it's time for you to start!" joked Jerry. "You've got to carry your weight, you know."

Rick didn't seem terribly amused, but pasted an obligatory grin on his face. Jerry continued, "Seriously, the Product Owner has a crucial role in Scrum. Sure, the team will self-organize and become a well-oiled machine, but, as they say, 'garbage in, garbage out.'"

"What do you mean exactly?" Rick asked.

"You give them the direction. You tell them what needs to be done. A common failing in Scrum is a Product Owner with not enough knowledge to define and not enough authority to defend the backlog."

Rick bristled a bit. "I'm pretty sure I can handle that."

"You are?"

"Well, I've already made a project plan; we'll just cut it into two-week Sprints! After this Sprint, we'll have the automated testing in place. So after that we won't have to worry about quality; that will be baked in. I'll just feed the team everything on my schedule in small portions. I've got your whole backlog figured out and ready to go for the entire project." He sat back in his chair, emitting a cloud of self-satisfaction.

I sat forward quickly and steepled my fingers on my chin for a moment. "Rick," I paused for a second and let his attention focus on me, "I don't think you really grasp your new role here."

At that he started to sit up straight.

"Listen, you're just forcing your old process into the new one. That's serving new wine in old bottles and it just isn't going to work." I let the last few words come out slowly, each one sounding like a sentence in itself. "Throw away your plan."

"But Mark, I worked on that for months!"

I slapped the table. "And where did it get us, Rick? Where did it get us? I thought you had a glimmer of the scope of the change we needed to make, dammit!"

He rocked back, startled.

"Listen, Rick, we do not need, or want, to look ahead in that kind of detail. You've got to let it go. We need to get in close with Logistrux and get their feedback so it informs us where to go next. Together we can determine which things will add the highest value to the customer. Do you know what those features are? Do you?"

"No, but…"

"Neither do I. We need to find out! Then we can build the backlog for the next Sprint. Then after this Sprint, we work with them again, and Sprint by Sprint we get closer to what they want! C'mon, Rick, haven't you been paying attention? Your old plan is dead!" With that I grabbed his laptop and threw it across the room. It crunched into the drywall and hung there, half in and half out of the wall.

The sound hit both of us like a slap. The two of us stared at the laptop for a moment, expecting it to fall. Instead it hung there, not even quivering. I fell back down into my chair.

Jerry cleared his throat. "Here's what might help, Rick." We both turned toward him; we'd forgotten he was in the room. "Think of it this way. Detailing what you're going to do in the future doesn't make a lot of sense; it's a waste of time. The details that you need will arise as they are needed, as a natural part of the process. A lot of details you think you need now, you'll realize later are completely irrelevant. The problem is that you've been taught that you have to think out every-thing beforehand. That's just good planning, am I right?"

Rick's breathing slowed a bit from the emotional peak he'd been at. Jerry's jocular and melodious tone took all the bite out of what he was saying. "I guess."

Jerry nodded enthusiastically. "Exactly. We were all taught that. It's wrong, though. First, you can't get any feedback in advance, so you won't know if what you're making is what the customer actu-ally wants. Second, the world is changing constantly, so things that seem right now like they will be really important in two months may be completely irrelevant by then. If you freeze your backlog in detail, plan the whole thing out, it's like putting your head in the sand. You're making up the whole thing. You're basing your work on a world that doesn't exist yet! That's crazy!"

Jerry's excitement was almost palpable. "If, though, you continu-ously adapt your business case as you realize it, you can use feedback from the real world to change that business case. And the more often you do that, the better that business case is going to be. During the project, you must always be prepared to change direction, to be agile. And it's your job as the Product Owner to make that kind of call."

Jerry took one of his meticulously measured sips of coffee. I imag-ined him at home using a pipette to measure his dosage. "Here's what happens if you plan too far ahead: you'll be constantly weighing all the details in your plan. I'm sure you've had conversations with your-self like, 'Well, I can't implement this current feature this way, because in a few months we have to integrate this other feature that works in a different way.' Am I wrong?"

"No, I've done exactly that."

"And that's your mistake. Don't do that. What is important now is more important than what's in the future; that's what prioritizing your backlog does. If you don't do that, you're reversing your priorities! The goal of prioritization is doing the important stuff first. By the time you get to the stuff later on down the line, it may not even be necessary anymore—and meanwhile, you've wasted time now for something you will never do."

Jerry's enthusiastic tone dropped for a moment. "This is really important, Rick. You have to let go of your old ways of doing things. If you don't, if you can't abandon thinking too far ahead, you will not succeed with Scrum. I've seen organizations paralyze themselves over this and not be able to make the transition. They fear the unknown. But you have to do the opposite." The enthusiasm crept back into his voice, like he just couldn't help it. "Embrace the unknown! That's where learning lies! If you're too afraid to learn, you will never get any better. This is the key to being successful at Scrum: embrace change."

Rick was silent for a moment. I looked at the laptop still hanging in the wall before I spoke. "Rick. I know you've told me that you can do this, that you can make this change. I need you to live up to that. I need you to look me in the eye and tell me you can do it. If you can't abandon your current mindset, well, this is the time to say so. This project needs a good Product Owner. This team needs one. I need you to help and guide them in order to make this project successful."

Rick looked at me. I felt all the anger drain out of me, leaving me exhausted. "The customer is Logistrux. I need you to work with them—closely. They can give us the answers to a lot of our problems, but you have to give up your belief that you already know those answers. You don't. I don't. But you have to have faith in your team. You have to have faith in yourself. Whatever comes up, you can handle it. Any change, embrace it, bring it in, make it your friend. But you only do that at the start of each Sprint, when we require planning; not before, not after. Got it?"

There was silence. Rick knew, and I knew, his job was on the line. Not in three months, but in three minutes. It was now or never. He glanced at the laptop. I noted to myself that throwing things into walls, while perhaps not the best choice, certainly got people's attention.

Rick blew out some air, took a deep breath. "Okay. I'm an idiot. I get that. I'm doing it again, aren't I? Just like I did as a project manager, what, last week? I'm just trying to avoid problems and risk by planning ahead, but you know that. I'm making myself more important than the team. If there are problems, I try to solve them myself, instead of working to prevent those problems in the first place. And you're right; I've been more focused on preventing problems than finding out what Logistrux needs."

He looked down at the table. You could feel the tension leaving the room. My shoulders started to relax as I realized I wasn't going to have to fire Rick today.

"I can see it now." Rick said. "I was sending documents to Logistrux, but never really talking to them, never really bringing them on board. No wonder they never responded." Rick looked up at me, and then to Jerry. "And to be honest, I'm not sure if I ever really wanted a response. That would have disturbed the precious schedule I'd spent so much time on. Feedback only required more work, more planning."

I was about to say something when Rick held up his hand. "No, let me finish. Every time I had to redo the plan just made more work. I never should have planned that far ahead or in that much detail. What I envisioned the product to be became more important than what Logistrux wanted. I get it. Any feedback coming from them is much more important than what was in my plan. They were the ones who were actually using and buying the product! Jesus, I feel stupid. I worked harder and harder, but made the problem worse."

He locked his gaze with mine. "I've already apologized to you once, Mark. I'm going to try not to have to make a habit of it. But I'm sorry. I know I have to do things differently." He turned toward Jerry. "All right, what does a good backlog look like? What should and shouldn't be on it? What do I need to do differently?"

Jerry smiled, excited by Rick's change of heart. I noticed he carefully avoided looking at the laptop stuck in the wall. "A good backlog, like most things, depends on the situation. It's different for every organization, every application domain, and every product and maturity stage of a product. But there are some general rules."

He got up and moved to the whiteboard. He had to avoid the laptop, but instead of walking around it, and still without looking at it, he wiggled it free from the wall and put it on the table. He started writing on the whiteboard.

"First, a backlog shouldn't be too detailed too far ahead. You really shouldn't refine a backlog more than two Sprints ahead, and even then you should be prepared to change it. Because what you want is feedback from the customer from the results of each Sprint. That feedback is going to demand adjustments, and those changes in priority will probably make some things you now think are important, irrelevant."

Rick calmly said, "I hear you, Jerry, but how does that work in the long term? We have to be careful that the product is maintainable, consistent, scalable, all those kind of things. If the team only addresses the top few priorities, aren't we in danger of losing focus on the big picture?"

"I hear your concerns, Rick," Jerry replied. "What you want is for you and the team to have a good overview on both the how and the why of the product. You're right, that's critical. You should expect to consider architecture, vision, future flexibility. But as you assess each Sprint to see what you're contributing to the overall vision, this approach is still effective. Why? Because architecture evolves. It isn't something you can pin down beforehand. You define your architectural vision for the product, but you have to be able to adapt that vision as you get more information."

Jerry sat back down. "Look at it this way. If you build the uncertainty of the future into your architecture, you're going to be less constrained by past decisions when you inevitably have to change things. So, **the things that add the most value for your customer you do first, without thought of future things that add less value. You may never have to do those things.** This is the essence, and I know it's completely different than what you've been doing. **Adding the most value in the shortest time should always be your goal.**"

"And those things that are less important than you thought? You don't build them. You only build exactly the right things. The profit from that alone far outweighs any gains you might have made by trying to anticipate all future scenarios."

"Okay, second rule." Jerry bounced back up. "It comes out of the first one. **A backlog shows an overall vision of the future, but not a detailed one. You only detail the next couple of Sprints, but you do define your vision in a broad way. You express in chunks of increasing size what may come later.** That way the team knows how the current Sprint fits into the bigger picture. The product backlog defines that overall vision, so it has to include all the ideas, strategic or not, for the product. But, it is prioritized on added value; the lower the value, the farther out in time it is. The common term used is 'granularity.' In essence, it means that the degree of detail in a product backlog, the 'granularity,' if you will, decreases as you look farther ahead in time. Sometimes—heck, often—you'll never have to do some of those things on the far end of the time horizon, so you shouldn't waste the energy of working out all the details."

"Maybe I'm just being slow here," Rick said carefully, "but if we don't capture things in detail, how does the team know what to do? I'm not asking because I don't want to do it"—his eyes quickly shifted toward me, then back to Jerry—"but just because I want to understand. I just don't get how things will run well if we don't make it crystal clear what we need."

Jerry replied instantly, "Good question. And you'll be happy to know that many Product Owners struggle with it. Here's what you do: don't work out how something will be done. That will be taken care of during the Sprint. **Your job as Product Owner is to put the what, the why, and for whom it is important in the backlog. In other words, you set the context within which the team can figure out the best solution. The 'why' is really important, because that communicates the value of the backlog item.** And if you don't communicate the value to the team, the team just has to guess what it is when making technical choices. And guess what? Often they'll guess wrong. That's why you, as the Product Owner, need to explain the what, the why, and for whom."

"Here, let me show you something." With that Jerry got up and walked back to the whiteboard, talking as he began to erase the board. "Often software requirements are defined in terms of 'solutions.' That's a mistake. Everything is specified in detail down to screens and buttons. The developers are given something they only have to build. This doesn't use even half of the talents and skills of a developer. You, as the Product Owner, are saying that you, alone, are smart enough to figure out the optimal solution to every problem. That's just hubris."

He stopped, the board cleared. "So how do we do it in Scrum? Well, instead of supplying solutions, you provide…you might say 'value requests,' or what we like to call 'user stories'. They describe a scenario that defines the what and the why, but NOT the how. The 'how' is the province of the software engineers; that's why you hired them, and the Product Owner shouldn't interfere."

"Here's what one looks like," he began to write on the board. "As a 'role' - - the for whom I want to 'take action' - the what so that I 'reach a certain value' - the why."

He quickly wrote a few examples on the board.

User Story Examples:

As a <u>user</u> I want to <u>access our schedules in the system, when not connected to the network,</u> so that I <u>can work while on the move and can make direct promises during customer meetings so I can close deals immediately.</u>

As a <u>member of the management team,</u> I want to <u>be able to demonstrate new functionality to potential customers</u> so that I <u>can convince them that their requests are on the way so that I can win deals earlier and easier.</u>

As an <u>account manager</u> I want to <u>start up our product within a single second</u> so that I <u>can impress potential customers with our product performance as this makes closing deals much easier.</u>

I thought about the idea for a moment, then spoke. "This is as granular as a user story gets? That doesn't make any sense. How does such an abstract description help a team perform better? Won't there be too many ambiguities and misunderstandings for the team to be efficient? Wouldn't it be better to write down what's needed in more detail?"

"Absolutely right." Jerry grinned at me. "It doesn't seem to be the most efficient way, does it? But efficiency isn't the key to speedy delivery. Effectiveness and understanding of the situation are far more decisive factors in the speed of the process. Focus on becoming totally effective and you'll receive efficiency with it for free! The great thing about user stories is that they aren't complete."

He saw that Rick and I were still a little lost. "Okay, answer me this: what do you think developers do when they see one of these stories?"

I had only started to consider the question when Rick leapt in. "That's easy! They'll ask the Product Owner what it means precisely. I get it! A conversation is started between the Product Owner and developer and they both learn from it." Jerry started to talk, but Rick spoke over him. "But I think it would be even better to have those discussions with Logistrux, no? They're the ones actually using the product. Now that I think about it, we need to talk to Logistrux right away so we can actually get those stories right, rather than just guess based on what we think is right. They are going to tell us the 'whys'!"

He was right, I realized. He had just nailed why we had been failing. We didn't really know their requirements. We thought we knew them—they'd even been written down—but we hadn't bothered to ask Logistrux to point out which of the conclusions we'd reached were wrong. After all, getting their input would have disrupted our planning. We should have been talking to them all along.

I leaned back in my chair as Rick and Jerry continued to talk about user stories. God damn it. How many times had thirty pages of specifications been treated like holy writ, not ever to be questioned, even if we knew they included assumptions and inaccuracies? Even doing Scrum, we were still making the same mistake. We still hadn't had a real conversation with Logistrux! I was an idiot.

"Rick," I interrupted them. "You need to be in London by tomorrow morning. Fly out tonight."

Rick grinned; he'd said he wanted to travel more. "I don't think that will be a problem at home if it's only for a few days."

Jerry said he'd like to go as well to work with Rick on his new role and help him develop a backlog of good user stories. Rick called Logistrux, and they booked themselves on the 1:30 p.m. flight to Heathrow.

As they bustled out of the office, buzzing with excitement, I turned to my next challenge. There were only a few days until my wedding anniversary. I wasn't sure what story I'd come up with. Maybe something like: "As a husband, I want to stay married so we can be happy like we used to be." Hmm. I thought maybe Keats would work better.

the**essentials**

1

The Product Owner is crucial for effective Scrum. Even a team with a great working process will still suffer from "garbage in, garbage out."

2

The Product Owner role is the most difficult and least understood role in Scrum. If the Product Owner doesn't have the authority, or simply lacks sufficient knowledge, she won't be able to decide on product backlog issues, and the Scrum implementation will fail.

3

Time. Time spent training, coaching, and learning is needed to speed up the adoption of new roles, and more significantly, the new mindset

4

The Product Owner must ensure that a backlog does not describe "solutions," but instead it lists "value requests." In Scrum this is done using "user stories" that describes a usage scenario and setting. It describes the *what*, the *for whom*, and the value of that scenario: the *why*.

5

Based on a set of user-stories team members request details from the Product Owner. Both the Product Owner and the developers learn from those discussions, which are actually more important than the story itself.

6

A backlog holds the vision for the future. It provides a "destination on the horizon." The product backlog contains all the ideas, whether strategic or not. They are then prioritized in terms of value. The further away in time they lie, the more abstractly they are described.

7

A more detailed description is usually only needed for stories two Sprints out.

8

First, do what adds the most value.

Chapter 9:
Sprint Finalization

...

I drove home that night with some excitement. Throwing that laptop into the wall had… I don't know… freed me somehow. I felt different, like I had broken through a wall, a pattern of behavior that had been keeping me going down the same path, repeating things in the same pattern. I hadn't always been like that. It was like the customary thing to do, the "right" way of doing things, had slowly wrapped around me in layers, each successive one numbing me, making it harder to move, to see things clearly, to do things that just worked!

It felt like I had ripped off those layers. The world seemed sharper, fresher "Anne!" I yelled as I walked in the door. "Guess what I did today?"

She was standing in the kitchen holding a glass of wine. She seemed a bit startled by my enthusiasm. "What?"

"I threw a laptop into a wall!"

"You what?"

"And it stuck."

"What?"

"Seriously," I imitated my throwing motion from earlier. "I picked it up and spun it into the wall like a Frisbee. And it stuck there. Its edge went far enough in that it hung there. It was wild."

"Why did you throw a laptop into the wall?" she asked carefully.

"And the best part was, no one even mentioned it. They were so startled—it came at them so out of left field—that they couldn't come up with a verbal response."

"Mark, why did you throw a laptop into the wall?" She set her wine glass down and looked at me, concerned.

"Because Rick was stuck. He couldn't change. I had to do something drastic. It was change or die." I stopped.

"How did he take it?"

"I think he's going to change. I think," I said. "I hope. It's hard to change. I remember my mother once talking to my nephew. He was maybe three years old. I can't remember what it was about, but he was in full meltdown mode. Tears, sobbing, the whole bit. I think it was because plans had changed in one way or another; he couldn't go to the park or something. And she said something that stuck with me then, and it stuck with him, 'Change is hard.' I'll never forget that: change is hard. Even when it's the right thing to do, even when it's what you have to do, that doesn't make it any easier. It is hard."

I poured myself a glass of wine and carefully didn't look at her. "Look at us. We have to change. We've been dancing around what's been happening at my work for months now. It's driving us crazy because we don't know how to really talk to each other in a new environment. And that's scary."

I looked at her. Her eyes were wet as she reached out and took my hand. "It is," she said. "It is scary."

"But I think we can do it. We've let circumstances change what we want to do, rather than imposing what we want on the world. We're worrying too much about the future, about what might go wrong, so we're not doing anything. Forget that. Forget whether it's the right time or the wrong time; let's just do it."

"Are you saying…?"

"Yes. Let's do it; let's start a family. I know things are a little crazy right now, but let's do it anyway. I think we can change enough—both now, and if things become even crazier in the future. Let's just say, 'We want this' and do it, come what may."

Anne smiled and her hand reached for mine.

"Come what may," She said. We left the kitchen then, and I'll end the blow by blow account there.

And with that, we had made a decision. That moment sticks with me even now. Making a decision, sticking with it and adapting to whatever happens. That's what makes us strong, both in our lives and in our work. But saying out loud that it isn't easy, acknowledging the fear and upset—that's the first step. Because change is hard.

. . .

A week later, Rick and Jerry got back from London with some good news. Rick had spent the time well, getting more and more detailed feedback and user stories from Logistrux. And having them there had sent the right message; the people at Logistrux now saw that we were giving this project the attention it deserved. Best of all, Rick came back with a clear idea of how Logistrux expected to make money with our software. He now knew what functionality was important to them, and why.

Rick returned with a list of thirty user stories. Some were abstract, but those were farther down on the backlog: things that could be worked out later before they were put on a Sprint backlog. But the items with the most value Rick had well in hand. He thought it would only take one Sprint to address the top five user stories. And with those we could deliver a version of the product to Logistrux that would instantly be able to deliver value to them.

Rick was curious as to how the rest of the Sprint had gone while he was away. I'd been at the daily stand ups and was pretty clued in as to what had been accomplished. We all came together at a meeting held at the end of our first Sprint. We'd learned from Jerry that sometimes it's called the 'Sprint Review Meeting,' or simply 'The Demo.' Everyone was there. Even some people from marketing and sales showed up. George felt comfortable enough in his role as Scrum Master that he told Jerry he wanted to lead the meeting. They worked on it together, but George took the lead. He was growing into his role.

During the first Sprint Review, the team demonstrated what they'd accomplished. As agreed, they'd disabled the Internet option and only supported one database type, the one that Logistrux used.

That was just fine. The team had completed the entire Sprint backlog and had largely completed the Definition of Done as well. The Scrum board had all the items in the right-hand "Done" column, and the burn-down chart neatly glided toward zero. There were a couple of loose ends, one part of the user manual still needed to be updated, and one feature hadn't been tested in time, but the Sprint had been a success.

Rick and Jerry were astonished. I was happy, but not as surprised; I'd been at the daily meetings and knew how smoothly things were going. Two weeks before, I had had a project without an end, an irate customer, and no idea of when we could deliver. Just two weeks later, we had a stable product with all the basic functionality, and we thought that with one more Sprint we could do a pre-release.

Rick was thrilled. He told the team that with the very first Sprint, we had already covered ninety percent of Logistrux's needs. He was eager to get going on the next Sprint to take care of that last ten percent.

After the demo, Jerry turned to Rick. They'd bonded over that week in London; you could tell it from their body language. I wondered if Rick had even copied Jerry's coffee process. "Rick, you're the Product Owner. Two weeks ago we put the team to work on the Sprint backlog; well, now you've seen the results. I just want to bring one thing up: remember that at the beginning of the Sprint, we asked each member of the team to give their commitment to the Sprint?"

Rick nodded. Jerry continued, "By giving their commitment, they officially took over responsibility for the project during the Sprint. In a way, they were the 'owners' of the product. Now it's important for you to officially take that responsibility back. You do that by dismissing the team, by accepting their work. This might seem a bit officious, but I find that doing this explicitly removes potential for confusion. It makes it crystal clear who is responsible for the product and when. So, we asked for explicit commitment from the team; now we ask you, explicitly:"Do you accept the Sprint result? Do we dismiss the team?"

"Definitely," Rick said, "This is great work, guys. Listen, Jerry and I just got back from Logistrux, and they made it clear how we can help them. I understand their business case even better; I think we can help a lot of our other clients with this functionality as well. So, Logistrux and Jerry and I put together a bunch of user stories. Of those, five are critical. But we already address a lot of them with what we have; I think with one more Sprint we can deliver a working version to them! That's what, two months ahead of schedule, Mark?"

"Fifty-five days early," I said, smiling. "You know, guys, just a few weeks ago I thought I might be looking for a new job. I felt like we had no control over our product or our processes. I don't feel that way anymore. What you've accomplished is incredible." I turned and met each of their eyes. "Thank you."

Jerry spoke up. "Thanks for those words, Mark and Rick, but before we get to planning the next Sprint, we need to finish this one. We still have the most important meeting of the Sprint to go: the Retrospective. This is where we talk about what worked and what didn't. Then we can figure out how we're going to approach the next Sprint, and what we should do differently, if anything. But first, let's have some lunch!"

As everyone started toward the sandwiches, one other silent member of the audience caught my eye: Dave. I was surprised he hadn't said a thing, as CEO; I wondered if he just didn't want anyone to be intimidated by what he had to say. He motioned me over and we stepped into the hall.

"Fifty-five days, Mark? Are you serious?"

"Listen, you've seen what this team can do in just two weeks."

"Doesn't work yet."

"But it will. Don't tell me that Logistrux is still pissed off."

"They're less…" He paused for a second reflecting on what word to use, and finally decided on "…incandescent. Less outraged—the trip out there did help—but they need to see real progress."

"They will."

"They'd better, Mark. I won't mention early delivery to them; I think you're going to need every day you have."

I looked at the floor for a second, then back up at him. "Say what you have to say. We'll be done."

Dave nodded and started to walk off before he turned and asked, "Did you really throw a laptop into a wall?"

I felt a flush in my cheeks."Yes."

"And it actually stuck there?"

"Yeah."

"Good; I think you really do understand the stakes here. About time you got fired up."

And with that he did walk away.

. . .

After lunch, Jerry called us all to order."An important part of Scrum is that we, as a team, own our own work processes."

Everyone was here, including George, Rick and me. Jerry had proposed leading this first Retrospective, because it was not only the most important meeting in Scrum, but the most difficult as well.

"As the owners of the process, you have to maintain it, as well as run it." Jerry had brought with him his inevitable coffee cup and took one of those precise sips. **"Too often I see organizations just continue doing what they're doing, without even thinking about how they entrap themselves in old ways of doing things that may not work going forward—without thinking about how they can do it better.** It's insane, but very human; change is hard, folks."

Jerry looked around the room,"But now you own the process. You have to make sure that your process is continually being optimized. In Scrum, this meeting, the Retrospective, is how we do that. We need to identify what went well, and how we can do those things better. But we also have to talk about what didn't go well, and how we can fix that."

Another sip."**The Retrospective is the most important meeting in Scrum. After all, this is where you can explicitly improve your processes—how you can get better! If you do Scrum well, each Sprint is better than the one before.** So the Retrospective is important, but it's also hard. I'll tell you why: because it requires honesty, openness, and mutual respect. All those things we pay lip service to, but we avoid in our day-to-day lives. Because it's scary. It makes you vulnerable. People don't like that. But if you want to get better, if you are actually committed to continuously improving, you've got to do it."

"A few things before we begin. First, the Retrospective is never about individual performance; it's about how the whole team performed, how the process performed. This isn't always easy, and if you're not careful it can turn personal. This is why a lot of organizations have problems with the Retrospective. Instead they use it as a casual get-together to tell each other how great they are. They don't improve. The core of the Retrospective is one thing: action! We have to improve the process, and it has to become part of how we work."

"The Retrospective is dependent on the Product Owner to focus it." He nodded toward Rick. "Today, I'll fill that role."

"Okay. A Retrospective begins with looking at the results of the last Retrospective; obviously we can't do that in this first one. But be sure you do it in the future! If there isn't enough follow-up from one Retrospective to another, there must be an agreement to put the decisions into the next Sprint. **If the Retrospective becomes nothing more than defining potential actions that aren't acted upon, it is useless. If the improvements identified in the Retrospective are not implemented, then Scrum fails! Without that implementation, there is no improvement; if there isn't continuous improvement, Scrum dies. That is the whole point: to get better!**"

Jerry, at times, seemed to vibrate with intensity. This was one of those times. You could feel the energy flickering off him. He seemed to calm for a moment, then spoke again.

"So, these actions we decide should be taken...they should be aimed at improving the outcome of each subsequent Sprint. They can include the quotidian, like 'I need a better mouse' or 'Let's cut down on the spelling mistakes in documentation.' But those are trivial, marginal at best; let's address them, by all means, but that's not what we're really after. In the Retrospective we want bigger ideas. The Scrum Master or Product Owner might say, 'During the next Sprint, we're going to double the quality of work,' or, 'Next Sprint we double our velocity and double our fun.' Then we focus everything on those goals, and what actions we need to take to get there. In Scrum, our dreams are not of small things. Let's make everything better, one Sprint at a time."

Jerry sipped his coffee again. "This Retrospective, we're just going to look back at this first Sprint. First, let's make a list of things that went well. Cherish those things that went well. Feel joyful about them, and let's see if we can make them even better. It's sometimes better to improve the things that you do well, rather than try to improve the things you don't. And then let's prioritize that list. What are the things that will have the most impact on our work and velocity? What should we really focus on?"

"And then"—Jerry stood and wrote "Good" on the whiteboard— "and then we turn to what improvements are actually going to be implemented. Remember, we're not here just to talk about what worked; we're here to take concrete action to make those things better. Then we do the same thing with the things that didn't go well. We list them, then prioritize them, and at the end of this Retrospective we should have a concrete list of things we can do to improve the Scrum process. A list of things we can take action on during the next Sprint. This is crucial, concrete action, not theoretical discussion."

And so on we went. Jerry led us through the process, and it was obvious this wasn't the first one of these he had done. He seemed to know instinctively when someone needed a bit more time, or someone else needed to be reined in. Because of his adept and respectful handling of the meeting, no one really minded that much when Jerry killed a discussion.

From the list the team came up with of things that went well, the only action that came forward was to expand the Definition of Done. From the things that went wrong, a couple of practical solutions emerged, like moving the standup to 9:30 to make sure everyone could be there on time. The team also decided to limit the number of items in the "Busy" column. They had learned that the more Busy items there were, the more stories failed in a Sprint. They agreed that no one should work on more than one work item at a time, and there were seven people on the team, so no more than seven sticky notes should be in the center. And those seven sticky notes should represent work on no more than three stories. Working from the top of the Scrum board and getting stories fully completed and tested as fast as possible made for a better Sprint and higher velocity.

Then we put all of these actions into the backlog and listed them on the Scrum board, so they would get the attention they deserved. This way, the team, Product Owner, and Scrum Master could monitor our progress and prioritize the actions needed. The team agreed to evaluate these items in the daily standup and in the next Sprint Retrospective.

After the Retrospective was finished, everyone talked for a few moments. I leaned back and looked at the team: at Rick, at George, at Jerry, and Susan. This group of people had done something extraordinary. They had changed how they worked, so they could do better. They had embraced the new, and saved the company they worked for.

George stood up and closed the meeting. "Okay, everyone be in the auditorium tomorrow morning at 9:30 sharp; Rick will present the new backlog. I am certainly interested in those five user stories."

I told everyone to meet me at the local watering hole after work. Drinks were on me. It's important to use every opportunity you can to gather as a team. Problems and challenges are always there, but times to bask in victory and reflect are rare. Celebrate them. It makes "fun" more fun.

Jeff Sutherland, Rini van Solingen, Eelco Rustenburg

the**essentials**

1
The Sprint review meeting is a live demonstration of the current state of the product, which should fully meet the Definition of Done. It is NOT a PowerPoint presentation or a demo that shows only the front end. It demonstrates progress on the basis of the real working software.

2
At the end of the demo, the Product Owner discharges the team, so they are free to make new commitments. This clarifies the responsibilities and ownership of the product.

3
An important part of Scrum is that the team owns its working processes and that those processes are continuously improved.

4
During the Retrospective, the team analyses how they did in the last Sprint, so they can improve on what went well AND address what didn't go well.

5
A Retrospective leads to action. The meeting has only one result: a list of concrete measures to structurally improve the Scrum process. The next Sprint should always be better, faster, and more fun than the previous one. It's not about working *harder*, it's about working *smarter!*

6
The Retrospective is often the most difficult meeting of all. Many organizations struggle to make this meeting successful. The primary impediment is the lack of training on how to give constructive, actionable feedback.

7
In the larger context, the Retrospective is much more than defining potential actions. If the improvements revealed by the Retrospective aren't implemented; there is no improvement between Sprints, and Scrum fails.

Chapter 10:
How the Story Ends

...

Rick's five most critical user stories turned out to be a touch bigger than a single Sprint; the team estimated it would take three. But two of the five could be done in one Sprint. After that Sprint, Rick went back to Logistrux with a working product. From the near death of the project to software that worked in a matter of weeks. They were impressed—and so was I.

Rick learned during his visit that Logistrux still needed some changes, but that was fine. We wanted changes from them; changes added value. And as we were addressing the highest value features first, coping with change was no problem. All work on the next Sprint had become completely flexible; in a way, it didn't matter to us what we were going to work on next. We knew that no matter what we did, it would be in alignment with what the customer actually wanted, not what we thought the customer wanted—and that would increase the value of the product for them.

Working in two-week Sprints worked well for us. A team can't really break that many things in two weeks. We also noticed that our product became more and more stable from one Sprint to the next. Automated testing helped with that, as did continuously checking quality. Now, every time a developer checked a file back into the version management system, the product was immediately built and fully tested automatically. The developer knew instantly whether her code worked. Bugs became much easier to find.

We used to spend time hunting for bugs that were introduced months ago. Now we tried to find and fix them immediately. The amount of time, money, and frustration saved was enormous.

In the months that followed the introduction of Scrum, it was amazing to watch it really fall into place. After the Christmas holidays, everyone walked back into the office, looked at the Scrum Board, knew instantly what the state of the project was, signed out the next item on the board, and went to work. It used to take a week to get everyone back up to speed after a break; now it just took an hour.

Logistrux was happy too. The new functionality dovetailed so perfectly with what they needed, it added immediate value to the product. One month after receiving the results of the first Sprint, before we even delivered any sort of "final" product, they had increased their market share by ten percent, their biggest one-month growth ever. That kind of result made them happy with us, with the team, and with me. That's what we wanted to do: add real value for our customers. Have a real impact on their business. A few months later, we rolled the product out to all of our customers, and pretty soon it wasn't just Logistrux who was happy with us. It was a golden opportunity for our company.

We're still using Scrum. It's standard practice throughout the company. Even in Sales and Marketing, and our C-level corporate team. We've reduced the team size a bit, to seven. We've found that size works for us best; there are fewer "lines" within a team, and we can almost always squeeze everyone into a single office. If a project requires more people, we split it up into smaller projects, and smaller still, until there is a workload that seven people can handle.

George is still a Scrum Master; he now leads the Scrum of Scrums, helping the other Scrum Masters work together. And Vince, who so memorably blew up at one of the early meetings, is now a Scrum Master. He's even enthusiastic about the daily stand-ups!

The Scrum of Scrums is the daily meeting of all the Scrum Masters, immediately after the stand-ups with their own teams. In that meeting they discuss impediments and dependencies between teams and help each other out. They occasionally need my help, but not often now.

I've been able to pull myself out of managing the details of the product and focus more on strategy: spending more time with customers and clients, figuring out what they'll need months down the line, or what our next product should be. We have five Product Owners now; Rick is still one of them. To create the product backlog and to capture the user stories, they also use Scrum, Sprinting at the same pace as the teams. I'm what they call the "Strategic Product Owner," involved in backlogs of three to thirteen months—only rough items of course, not in the details; those are addressed later only when we have to.

I do still participate in the End-of-Sprint meetings. That's where the finished product is demonstrated; that's where all the visions and strategy become reality. I have to be at those meetings!

Recently, I've been looking back and trying to figure out why our adoption of Scrum worked so well. The answer I've come up with is simple: we just started. We didn't delay, we didn't get into massive preparations, we didn't dither about it. We just did it. There are plenty of opportunities to adjust and plan within Scrum, so there is no reason to wait or prepare. "Not planning far ahead" is applicable not only to developing a product; it works in deploying Scrum itself. One of the critical moments was when Rick realized he had to switch his mindset, that he had to stop his rigorous planning and reversing priorities. I think that was the turning point. Never underestimate the power of a well-thrown laptop. When I talk to other CTO's about introducing Scrum, that's what I tell them to do—not the laptop, but **not looking too far ahead. I tell them to embrace change and rely on themselves and their team; that's when they'll reap the full rewards of Scrum**.

There are some preconditions for rolling out Scrum, though: two major ones in our experience. The first is that there really must be a team—a team that has members who are prepared to work for and with each other, a team willing to continually improve itself and its process. Just like a sports team that is committed to performing better every day. This requires that everyone subordinate themselves to the team, and that takes a certain mindset, a certain character, and usually, a cultural change. This isn't easy to do. There are always insecurities and egos that can get in the way. Scrum makes a lack of team spirit painfully obvious. Resistance is inevitable, like with Vince or Rick.

We've learned that we have to give people the chance and the time to make Scrum their own, and let them adopt it at their own pace.

The second precondition is having good Product Owners. Product Owners have to have sufficient authority to make decisions by themselves, have enough vision to define the product, and have enough leadership to deliver results. Ideally they're good at everything. They need to have enough management skills to know what they can do themselves and what they need to delegate. They need leadership, vision, and a deep knowledge of the product, combined with the ability to prioritize and make decisions. Such people are very rare and need to be developed.

Product Owners like that are able to make good product backlogs. Giving a well-oiled Scrum team a good backlog can make the impossible happen. We've seen that a few times ourselves. It's amazing!

Jerry left us after three months. His job was done. In the first few Sprints, his aid was invaluable to help us master Scrum. But after four Sprints, the team took up the rhythm themselves. Jerry actually got bored the last month. He wasn't needed, as the teams, with the help of the Scrum Masters, managed themselves. He had time to spare.

After he left, he wrote a book on how to apply Scrum more broadly, with multiple teams, or teams in multiple locations—even off-shore. How management needs requirements to be structured for multiple teams, and how strategy and operations need to cooperate to align the multiple levels of backlogs. I can't wait to read it, as many of the case studies come from our Scrum implementation. The book will make Scrum more transparent, in particular how you can let Scrum work to your advantage. **After all, you *need* to let Scrum work to your advantage. It's important to tune Scrum to your situation, your products, your clients, and your challenges. That will improve the results for your customers, and delivering added value to them is your ultimate goal!**

We still see Jerry every now and then. We regularly hold a Retrospective on the introduction of Scrum into our company, and how it's going. We do this because we use Scrum to introduce Scrum. This Scrum cycle lasts three months, so we see Jerry every quarter during the Retrospective. I think he likes it because he gets to see his little girl regularly. I wouldn't be surprised if he hustled some more business in the DC area soon.

And what happened to me?

Well, most importantly, I'm the father of a little girl now. And while I'm sure you might think your child is the most beautiful, smart, graceful, cutest thing on the planet, I hate to break it to you; you're wrong. Mine is. Being a parent is the most exhausting and exhilarating thing I've ever done.

I also had the pleasure of walking into Dave's office just a few weeks after we'd last talked, after that first retrospective when he had been so doubtful, and demoed the software for him.

"Okay, full functionality will only be 25 days early."

Dave looked at me for a long moment. "I can live with that."

"Good."

"And, yes."

"And, yes what?"

"You can have a raise."

He smiled at me. And that's when it really hit me. The team actually had pulled it off. We weren't all going to be fired.

"And the team?"

He smiled again. "I think we can work out some sort of bonus structure. I'll get back to you in…hmm…two weeks sound good?"

I was still laughing when I left his office.

I'm also writing a book currently, on how to apply Scrum outside of the software world. **You can use Scrum for all kinds of projects. Making a first version of the final product quickly, adding highest value first, arranging for early and regular feedback, and embracing changes from clients are the keys to success for almost any project!**

I've renovated my whole house using Scrum, managing all the construction workers using a Scrum-like approach. I knew I had to remake a spare bedroom into a nursery and make the place a little more child-friendly, so I drew the backlog up on one wall and every day had a standup meeting with all of them. It worked great! Construction workers, I noticed, don't think of jobs of two hours. They make a plan for one day and if it isn't finished, wrap it up the next, delaying the whole schedule by a day. With Scrum, we identified the feasibility of tasks much earlier and were able to move work between them. They also rarely finish things; they don't think in terms of the final product. This means all the rooms are finished at the last moment. With Scrum I encouraged them to make a difference every day; to actually finish something. Each room needed to be finished completely as soon as possible; after that the room could be "locked," because it was "done." Working toward a finished product always works well, even if that product is an individual room.

I strongly believe that we can use Scrum extensively outside of the software world. The construction industry is one possibility, but I also see opportunities in business services, the retail sector, health care, and so on. Every domain can benefit from rapid feedback and prioritization of value.

Are you working in an environment that uses large schedules covering long periods? Or working with processes that obtain feedback only at the end? Or where changes are made without it being clear what their value is and whether that value will actually be delivered?

Then Scrum is worth considering. In Scrum you only do that which adds the most value, and you get rapid feedback on whether it has fulfilled the requirements. When it doesn't, adapt this item first. When it does, close the item and move on to the next thing that adds the most value. This principle applies everywhere money is earned, customers are helped, or products are delivered.

the**essentials**

1

Scrum puts emphasis on quickly delivering the most added value

Prioritize your work based on added value. That which adds most value for your customer you do first, and you release a usable version as soon as possible. This way, your product will start to add value for your customer immediately.

1

Scrum provides quality, transparency and predictability

Scrum ensures that, through short iterations with a fixed lead time, you can deliver your product (according to your promises) as often as possible. Short iterations that each create a complete and releasable product are an important foundation for lasting relationships with customers because you consistently fulfill your promises. Moreover, quality increases and is proven over and over with each iteration.

3

Scrum stimulates early feedback

Scrum works because an evolutionary and experimental model with a short feedback loop is the most appropriate way to achieve good results. It is naive to think that you can have the best ideas beforehand, that you will need to specify first and subsequently only build and test. That idea should be abandoned: beforehand you should know the best direction, but you can never know the exact detailed outcome.

4

Scrum ensures that everyone is happy doing what they are good at

Scrum is fun for all concerned, because it creates a combination of team ownership, team performance, and team responsibility, and it keeps the process simple. It addresses the talents of software engineers in the right way. It create strictness where it must and freedom where it can.

5

Scrum is a matter of just going for it: You can start with Scrum immediately

You can make the transition to Scrum at any time. It is just a matter of mindset. Accept that only the near future can be specified and planned in detail, and you can start with Scrum today.

Acknowledgments

...

Publishing a book is always the result of teamwork. As such, we would like to thank everyone who directly or indirectly contributed to this one.

We would like to express our thanks explicitly to:

- Dick Stegeman for his inspiration and stimulation to write this book, from the first initial drafts to the final Dutch, French, German, and now also English version of this book.
- JJ Sutherland for editing the English version of our manuscript, vastly improving the story and its readability.
- Arline Sutherland for being a first time publisher and managing all the hassle.
- All reviewers for reading and commenting on earlier versions of this manuscript: Beste Altinay, Dick Stegeman, Mark van Dijk, Jarl Meijer, and many others.
- John Numan for his willingness to promote this book within Pearson Education, which resulted in the Dutch, German, and French version. Thanks for your collaboration and openness; it's a joy working with you. Also thanks for letting us publish this English version by ourselves.
- Cerion Armour-Brown for his editing work on an earlier English version of this manuscript. Thanks for removing the Dutch from our English.
- All of our colleagues at Xebia, Prowareness, Delft University of Technology, and Scrum Inc. for their support in the publishing and promotion of this book.
- Finally, our home fronts for their support and tolerance of the countless hours we spent working at the kitchen table.
- **and the countless others – you know who you are!**

About the authors

...

Jeff Sutherland is the co-creator of Scrum and the leading expert on how the framework has evolved to meet the needs of today's business. The vast majority of software development companies around the world use the methodology he developed in 1993 and formalized in 1995 with Ken Schwaber. As the CEO of Scrum Inc (www.scruminc.com) and the Senior Advisor and Agile Coach to OpenView Venture Partners he continues to share best practices with organizations around the globe and has written extensively on Scrum rules and methods. Jeff can be reached at jeff@scruminc.com.

Rini van Solingen is a part-time professor in Global Software Engineering at Delft University of Technology and is Chief Technology Officer at Prowareness (www.scrum.nl). He is an expert in product, process, and performance improvement of software and systems development. He also serves as the CTO of Prowareness. Rini can be reached at rini@scrum.nl.

Eelco Rustenburg heads the Agile Consulting & Training unit at Xebia (xebia.com), the leading Dutch Agile company. In addition to training with Jeff, he frequently moderates workshops with management teams and holds positions in esteemed steering groups for Agile adoption programs. Eelco can be reached at erustenburg@xebia.com.

Made in the USA
Lexington, KY
02 November 2012